C-592

T0344753

THIS IS YOUR **PASSBOOK**® FOR ...

PLUMBER'S HELPER

NLC®

NATIONAL LEARNING CORPORATION®

passbooks.com

COPYRIGHT NOTICE

This book is SOLELY intended for, is sold ONLY to, and its use is RESTRICTED to individual, bona fide applicants or candidates who qualify by virtue of having seriously filed applications for appropriate license, certificate, professional and/or promotional advancement, higher school matriculation, scholarship, or other legitimate requirements of educational and/or governmental authorities.

This book is NOT intended for use, class instruction, tutoring, training, duplication, copying, reprinting, excerption, or adaptation, etc., by:

1) Other publishers
2) Proprietors and/or Instructors of «Coaching» and/or Preparatory Courses
3) Personnel and/or Training Divisions of commercial, industrial, and governmental organizations
4) Schools, colleges, or universities and/or their departments and staffs, including teachers and other personnel
5) Testing Agencies or Bureaus
6) Study groups which seek by the purchase of a single volume to copy and/or duplicate and/or adapt this material for use by the group as a whole without having purchased individual volumes for each of the members of the group
7) Et al.

Such persons would be in violation of appropriate Federal and State statutes.

PROVISION OF LICENSING AGREEMENTS. — Recognized educational, commercial, industrial, and governmental institutions and organizations, and others legitimately engaged in educational pursuits, including training, testing, and measurement activities, may address request for a licensing agreement to the copyright owners, who will determine whether, and under what conditions, including fees and charges, the materials in this book may be used them. In other words, a licensing facility exists for the legitimate use of the material in this book on other than an individual basis. However, it is asseverated and affirmed here that the material in this book CANNOT be used without the receipt of the express permission of such a licensing agreement from the Publishers. Inquiries re licensing should be addressed to the company, attention rights and permissions department.

All rights reserved, including the right of reproduction in whole or in part, in any form or by any means, electronic or mechanical, including photocopying, recording, or by any information storage and retrieval system, without permission in writing from the Publisher.

Copyright © 2018 by

NLC®

National Learning Corporation

212 Michael Drive, Syosset, NY 11791
(516) 921-8888 • www.passbooks.com
E-mail: info@passbooks.com

PUBLISHED IN THE UNITED STATES OF AMERICA

PASSBOOK® SERIES

THE *PASSBOOK® SERIES* has been created to prepare applicants and candidates for the ultimate academic battlefield – the examination room.

At some time in our lives, each and every one of us may be required to take an examination – for validation, matriculation, admission, qualification, registration, certification, or licensure.

Based on the assumption that every applicant or candidate has met the basic formal educational standards, has taken the required number of courses, and read the necessary texts, the *PASSBOOK® SERIES* furnishes the one special preparation which may assure passing with confidence, instead of failing with insecurity. Examination questions – together with answers – are furnished as the basic vehicle for study so that the mysteries of the examination and its compounding difficulties may be eliminated or diminished by a sure method.

This book is meant to help you pass your examination provided that you qualify and are serious in your objective.

The entire field is reviewed through the huge store of content information which is succinctly presented through a provocative and challenging approach – the question-and-answer method.

A climate of success is established by furnishing the correct answers at the end of each test.

You soon learn to recognize types of questions, forms of questions, and patterns of questioning. You may even begin to anticipate expected outcomes.

You perceive that many questions are repeated or adapted so that you can gain acute insights, which may enable you to score many sure points.

You learn how to confront new questions, or types of questions, and to attack them confidently and work out the correct answers.

You note objectives and emphases, and recognize pitfalls and dangers, so that you may make positive educational adjustments.

Moreover, you are kept fully informed in relation to new concepts, methods, practices, and directions in the field.

You discover that you arre actually taking the examination all the time: you are preparing for the examination by "taking" an examination, not by reading extraneous and/or supererogatory textbooks.

In short, this PASSBOOK®, used directedly, should be an important factor in helping you to pass your test.

PLUMBER'S HELPER

DUTIES

Plumber's Helpers, under direct supervision, assist plumbers in the installation, maintenance and repair of piping and tubing for water, gas, waste, soil, fuel and vent lines. They assist plumbers in the installation of plumbing fixtures, including tanks, sprinklers and fire suppression systems; carry tools, working materials and equipment, and prepare same at the work locations; move heavy valves, piping and fixtures; cut, drill or otherwise prepare openings as may be necessary for installation, maintenance or repair of plumbing pipes or fixtures; use acetylene torches; cut and thread pipe with hand or electrically operated tools; clean-up work areas; and may operate a motor vehicle. All Plumber's Helpers perform related work.

SCOPE OF THE EXAMINATION

The multiple-choice test may include questions on: materials, piping, valves, fittings, supports, and other fixtures used in plumbing work; proper selection and use of tools and equipment used in the plumbing trade; installation and repairs of plumbing systems and fixtures; basic knowledge of the Plumbing Code; safe and proper work practices; basic customer service practices; and other related areas including written comprehension, written expression, problem sensitivity, mathematical reasoning, number facility, deductive reasoning, inductive reasoning, information ordering, spatial orientation, and attention to work.

HOW TO TAKE A TEST

I. YOU MUST PASS AN EXAMINATION

A. *WHAT EVERY CANDIDATE SHOULD KNOW*

Examination applicants often ask us for help in preparing for the written test. What can I study in advance? What kinds of questions will be asked? How will the test be given? How will the papers be graded?

As an applicant for a civil service examination, you may be wondering about some of these things. Our purpose here is to suggest effective methods of advance study and to describe civil service examinations.

Your chances for success on this examination can be increased if you know how to prepare. Those "pre-examination jitters" can be reduced if you know what to expect. You can even experience an adventure in good citizenship if you know why civil service exams are given.

B. *WHY ARE CIVIL SERVICE EXAMINATIONS GIVEN?*

Civil service examinations are important to you in two ways. As a citizen, you want public jobs filled by employees who know how to do their work. As a job seeker, you want a fair chance to compete for that job on an equal footing with other candidates. The best-known means of accomplishing this two-fold goal is the competitive examination.

Exams are widely publicized throughout the nation. They may be administered for jobs in federal, state, city, municipal, town or village governments or agencies.

Any citizen may apply, with some limitations, such as the age or residence of applicants. Your experience and education may be reviewed to see whether you meet the requirements for the particular examination. When these requirements exist, they are reasonable and applied consistently to all applicants. Thus, a competitive examination may cause you some uneasiness now, but it is your privilege and safeguard.

C. *HOW ARE CIVIL SERVICE EXAMS DEVELOPED?*

Examinations are carefully written by trained technicians who are specialists in the field known as "psychological measurement," in consultation with recognized authorities in the field of work that the test will cover. These experts recommend the subject matter areas or skills to be tested; only those knowledges or skills important to your success on the job are included. The most reliable books and source materials available are used as references. Together, the experts and technicians judge the difficulty level of the questions.

Test technicians know how to phrase questions so that the problem is clearly stated. Their ethics do not permit "trick" or "catch" questions. Questions may have been tried out on sample groups, or subjected to statistical analysis, to determine their usefulness.

Written tests are often used in combination with performance tests, ratings of training and experience, and oral interviews. All of these measures combine to form the best-known means of finding the right person for the right job.

II. HOW TO PASS THE WRITTEN TEST

A. *NATURE OF THE EXAMINATION*

To prepare intelligently for civil service examinations, you should know how they differ from school examinations you have taken. In school you were assigned certain definite pages to read or subjects to cover. The examination questions were quite detailed and usually emphasized memory. Civil service exams, on the other hand, try to discover your present ability to perform the duties of a position, plus your potentiality to learn these duties. In other words, a civil service exam attempts to predict how successful you will be. Questions cover such a broad area that they cannot be as minute and detailed as school exam questions.

In the public service similar kinds of work, or positions, are grouped together in one "class." This process is known as *position-classification*. All the positions in a class are paid according to the salary range for that class. One class title covers all of these positions, and they are all tested by the same examination.

B. *FOUR BASIC STEPS*

1) Study the announcement

How, then, can you know what subjects to study? Our best answer is: "Learn as much as possible about the class of positions for which you've applied." The exam will test the knowledge, skills and abilities needed to do the work.

Your most valuable source of information about the position you want is the official exam announcement. This announcement lists the training and experience qualifications. Check these standards and apply only if you come reasonably close to meeting them.

The brief description of the position in the examination announcement offers some clues to the subjects which will be tested. Think about the job itself. Review the duties in your mind. Can you perform them, or are there some in which you are rusty? Fill in the blank spots in your preparation.

Many jurisdictions preview the written test in the exam announcement by including a section called "Knowledge and Abilities Required," "Scope of the Examination," or some similar heading. Here you will find out specifically what fields will be tested.

2) Review your own background

Once you learn in general what the position is all about, and what you need to know to do the work, ask yourself which subjects you already know fairly well and which need improvement. You may wonder whether to concentrate on improving your strong areas or on building some background in your fields of weakness. When the announcement has specified "some knowledge" or "considerable knowledge," or has used adjectives like "beginning principles of..." or "advanced ... methods," you can get a clue as to the number and difficulty of questions to be asked in any given field. More questions, and hence broader coverage, would be included for those subjects which are more important in the work. Now weigh your strengths and weaknesses against the job requirements and prepare accordingly.

3) Determine the level of the position

Another way to tell how intensively you should prepare is to understand the level of the job for which you are applying. Is it the entering level? In other words, is this the position in which beginners in a field of work are hired? Or is it an intermediate or advanced level? Sometimes this is indicated by such words as "Junior" or "Senior" in the class title. Other jurisdictions use Roman numerals to designate the level – Clerk I, Clerk II, for example. The word "Supervisor" sometimes appears in the title. If the level is not indicated by the title, check the description of duties. Will you be working under very close supervision, or will you have responsibility for independent decisions in this work?

4) Choose appropriate study materials

Now that you know the subjects to be examined and the relative amount of each subject to be covered, you can choose suitable study materials. For beginning level jobs, or even advanced ones, if you have a pronounced weakness in some aspect of your training, read a modern, standard textbook in that field. Be sure it is up to date and has general coverage. Such books are normally available at your library, and the librarian will be glad to help you locate one. For entry-level positions, questions of appropriate difficulty are chosen – neither highly advanced questions, nor those too simple. Such questions require careful thought but not advanced training.

If the position for which you are applying is technical or advanced, you will read more advanced, specialized material. If you are already familiar with the basic principles of your field, elementary textbooks would waste your time. Concentrate on advanced textbooks and technical periodicals. Think through the concepts and review difficult problems in your field.

These are all general sources. You can get more ideas on your own initiative, following these leads. For example, training manuals and publications of the government agency which employs workers in your field can be useful, particularly for technical and professional positions. A letter or visit to the government department involved may result in more specific study suggestions, and certainly will provide you with a more definite idea of the exact nature of the position you are seeking.

III. KINDS OF TESTS

Tests are used for purposes other than measuring knowledge and ability to perform specified duties. For some positions, it is equally important to test ability to make adjustments to new situations or to profit from training. In others, basic mental abilities not dependent on information are essential. Questions which test these things may not appear as pertinent to the duties of the position as those which test for knowledge and information. Yet they are often highly important parts of a fair examination. For very general questions, it is almost impossible to help you direct your study efforts. What we can do is to point out some of the more common of these general abilities needed in public service positions and describe some typical questions.

1) General information

Broad, general information has been found useful for predicting job success in some kinds of work. This is tested in a variety of ways, from vocabulary lists to questions about current events. Basic background in some field of work, such as sociology or economics, may be sampled in a group of questions. Often these are principles which have become familiar to most persons through exposure rather than through formal training. It is difficult to advise you how to study for these questions; being alert to the world around you is our best suggestion.

2) Verbal ability

An example of an ability needed in many positions is verbal or language ability. Verbal ability is, in brief, the ability to use and understand words. Vocabulary and grammar tests are typical measures of this ability. Reading comprehension or paragraph interpretation questions are common in many kinds of civil service tests. You are given a paragraph of written material and asked to find its central meaning.

3) Numerical ability

Number skills can be tested by the familiar arithmetic problem, by checking paired lists of numbers to see which are alike and which are different, or by interpreting charts and graphs. In the latter test, a graph may be printed in the test booklet which you are asked to use as the basis for answering questions.

4) Observation

A popular test for law-enforcement positions is the observation test. A picture is shown to you for several minutes, then taken away. Questions about the picture test your ability to observe both details and larger elements.

5) Following directions

In many positions in the public service, the employee must be able to carry out written instructions dependably and accurately. You may be given a chart with several columns, each column listing a variety of information. The questions require you to carry out directions involving the information given in the chart.

6) Skills and aptitudes

Performance tests effectively measure some manual skills and aptitudes. When the skill is one in which you are trained, such as typing or shorthand, you can practice. These tests are often very much like those given in business school or high school courses. For many of the other skills and aptitudes, however, no short-time preparation can be made. Skills and abilities natural to you or that you have developed throughout your lifetime are being tested.

Many of the general questions just described provide all the data needed to answer the questions and ask you to use your reasoning ability to find the answers. Your best preparation for these tests, as well as for tests of facts and ideas, is to be at your physical and mental best. You, no doubt, have your own methods of getting into an exam-taking mood and keeping "in shape." The next section lists some ideas on this subject.

IV. KINDS OF QUESTIONS

Only rarely is the "essay" question, which you answer in narrative form, used in civil service tests. Civil service tests are usually of the short-answer type. Full instructions for answering these questions will be given to you at the examination. But in case this is your first experience with short-answer questions and separate answer sheets, here is what you need to know:

1) Multiple-choice Questions

Most popular of the short-answer questions is the "multiple choice" or "best answer" question. It can be used, for example, to test for factual knowledge, ability to solve problems or judgment in meeting situations found at work.

A multiple-choice question is normally one of three types—

- It can begin with an incomplete statement followed by several possible endings. You are to find the one ending which *best* completes the statement, although some of the others may not be entirely wrong.
- It can also be a complete statement in the form of a question which is answered by choosing one of the statements listed.
- It can be in the form of a problem – again you select the best answer.

Here is an example of a multiple-choice question with a discussion which should give you some clues as to the method for choosing the right answer:

When an employee has a complaint about his assignment, the action which will *best* help him overcome his difficulty is to
  A. discuss his difficulty with his coworkers
  B. take the problem to the head of the organization
  C. take the problem to the person who gave him the assignment
  D. say nothing to anyone about his complaint

In answering this question, you should study each of the choices to find which is best. Consider choice "A" – Certainly an employee may discuss his complaint with fellow employees, but no change or improvement can result, and the complaint remains unresolved. Choice "B" is a poor choice since the head of the organization probably does not know what assignment you have been given, and taking your problem to him is known as "going over the head" of the supervisor. The supervisor, or person who made the assignment, is the person who can clarify it or correct any injustice. Choice "C" is, therefore, correct. To say nothing, as in choice "D," is unwise. Supervisors have and interest in knowing the problems employees are facing, and the employee is seeking a solution to his problem.

2) True/False Questions

The "true/false" or "right/wrong" form of question is sometimes used. Here a complete statement is given. Your job is to decide whether the statement is right or wrong.

SAMPLE: A roaming cell-phone call to a nearby city costs less than a non-roaming call to a distant city.

This statement is wrong, or false, since roaming calls are more expensive.
This is not a complete list of all possible question forms, although most of the others are variations of these common types. You will always get complete directions for

answering questions. Be sure you understand *how* to mark your answers – ask questions until you do.

V. RECORDING YOUR ANSWERS

Computer terminals are used more and more today for many different kinds of exams.

For an examination with very few applicants, you may be told to record your answers in the test booklet itself. Separate answer sheets are much more common. If this separate answer sheet is to be scored by machine – and this is often the case – it is highly important that you mark your answers correctly in order to get credit.

An electronic scoring machine is often used in civil service offices because of the speed with which papers can be scored. Machine-scored answer sheets must be marked with a pencil, which will be given to you. This pencil has a high graphite content which responds to the electronic scoring machine. As a matter of fact, stray dots may register as answers, so do not let your pencil rest on the answer sheet while you are pondering the correct answer. Also, if your pencil lead breaks or is otherwise defective, ask for another.

Since the answer sheet will be dropped in a slot in the scoring machine, be careful not to bend the corners or get the paper crumpled.

The answer sheet normally has five vertical columns of numbers, with 30 numbers to a column. These numbers correspond to the question numbers in your test booklet. After each number, going across the page are four or five pairs of dotted lines. These short dotted lines have small letters or numbers above them. The first two pairs may also have a "T" or "F" above the letters. This indicates that the first two pairs only are to be used if the questions are of the true-false type. If the questions are multiple choice, disregard the "T" and "F" and pay attention only to the small letters or numbers.

Answer your questions in the manner of the sample that follows:

32. The largest city in the United States is
    A. Washington, D.C.
    B. New York City
    C. Chicago
    D. Detroit
    E. San Francisco

1) Choose the answer you think is best. (New York City is the largest, so "B" is correct.)
2) Find the row of dotted lines numbered the same as the question you are answering. (Find row number 32)
3) Find the pair of dotted lines corresponding to the answer. (Find the pair of lines under the mark "B.")
4) Make a solid black mark between the dotted lines.

VI. BEFORE THE TEST

Common sense will help you find procedures to follow to get ready for an examination. Too many of us, however, overlook these sensible measures. Indeed, nervousness and fatigue have been found to be the most serious reasons why applicants fail to do their best on civil service tests. Here is a list of reminders:

- Begin your preparation early – Don't wait until the last minute to go scurrying around for books and materials or to find out what the position is all about.
- Prepare continuously – An hour a night for a week is better than an all-night cram session. This has been definitely established. What is more, a night a week for a month will return better dividends than crowding your study into a shorter period of time.
- Locate the place of the exam – You have been sent a notice telling you when and where to report for the examination. If the location is in a different town or otherwise unfamiliar to you, it would be well to inquire the best route and learn something about the building.
- Relax the night before the test – Allow your mind to rest. Do not study at all that night. Plan some mild recreation or diversion; then go to bed early and get a good night's sleep.
- Get up early enough to make a leisurely trip to the place for the test – This way unforeseen events, traffic snarls, unfamiliar buildings, etc. will not upset you.
- Dress comfortably – A written test is not a fashion show. You will be known by number and not by name, so wear something comfortable.
- Leave excess paraphernalia at home – Shopping bags and odd bundles will get in your way. You need bring only the items mentioned in the official notice you received; usually everything you need is provided. Do not bring reference books to the exam. They will only confuse those last minutes and be taken away from you when in the test room.
- Arrive somewhat ahead of time – If because of transportation schedules you must get there very early, bring a newspaper or magazine to take your mind off yourself while waiting.
- Locate the examination room – When you have found the proper room, you will be directed to the seat or part of the room where you will sit. Sometimes you are given a sheet of instructions to read while you are waiting. Do not fill out any forms until you are told to do so; just read them and be prepared.
- Relax and prepare to listen to the instructions
- If you have any physical problem that may keep you from doing your best, be sure to tell the test administrator. If you are sick or in poor health, you really cannot do your best on the exam. You can come back and take the test some other time.

VII. AT THE TEST

The day of the test is here and you have the test booklet in your hand. The temptation to get going is very strong. Caution! There is more to success than knowing the right answers. You must know how to identify your papers and understand variations in the type of short-answer question used in this particular examination. Follow these suggestions for maximum results from your efforts:

1) Cooperate with the monitor

The test administrator has a duty to create a situation in which you can be as much at ease as possible. He will give instructions, tell you when to begin, check to see that you are marking your answer sheet correctly, and so on. He is not there to guard you, although he will see that your competitors do not take unfair advantage. He wants to help you do your best.

2) Listen to all instructions

Don't jump the gun! Wait until you understand all directions. In most civil service tests you get more time than you need to answer the questions. So don't be in a hurry. Read each word of instructions until you clearly understand the meaning. Study the examples, listen to all announcements and follow directions. Ask questions if you do not understand what to do.

3) Identify your papers

Civil service exams are usually identified by number only. You will be assigned a number; you must not put your name on your test papers. Be sure to copy your number correctly. Since more than one exam may be given, copy your exact examination title.

4) Plan your time

Unless you are told that a test is a "speed" or "rate of work" test, speed itself is usually not important. Time enough to answer all the questions will be provided, but this does not mean that you have all day. An overall time limit has been set. Divide the total time (in minutes) by the number of questions to determine the approximate time you have for each question.

5) Do not linger over difficult questions

If you come across a difficult question, mark it with a paper clip (useful to have along) and come back to it when you have been through the booklet. One caution if you do this – be sure to skip a number on your answer sheet as well. Check often to be sure that you have not lost your place and that you are marking in the row numbered the same as the question you are answering.

6) Read the questions

Be sure you know what the question asks! Many capable people are unsuccessful because they failed to *read* the questions correctly.

7) Answer all questions

Unless you have been instructed that a penalty will be deducted for incorrect answers, it is better to guess than to omit a question.

8) Speed tests

It is often better NOT to guess on speed tests. It has been found that on timed tests people are tempted to spend the last few seconds before time is called in marking answers at random – without even reading them – in the hope of picking up a few extra points. To discourage this practice, the instructions may warn you that your score will be "corrected" for guessing. That is, a penalty will be applied. The incorrect answers will be deducted from the correct ones, or some other penalty formula will be used.

9) Review your answers

If you finish before time is called, go back to the questions you guessed or omitted to give them further thought. Review other answers if you have time.

10) Return your test materials

If you are ready to leave before others have finished or time is called, take ALL your materials to the monitor and leave quietly. Never take any test material with you. The monitor can discover whose papers are not complete, and taking a test booklet may be grounds for disqualification.

VIII. EXAMINATION TECHNIQUES

1) Read the general instructions carefully. These are usually printed on the first page of the exam booklet. As a rule, these instructions refer to the timing of the examination; the fact that you should not start work until the signal and must stop work at a signal, etc. If there are any *special* instructions, such as a choice of questions to be answered, make sure that you note this instruction carefully.

2) When you are ready to start work on the examination, that is as soon as the signal has been given, read the instructions to each question booklet, underline any key words or phrases, such as *least, best, outline, describe* and the like. In this way you will tend to answer as requested rather than discover on reviewing your paper that you *listed without describing*, that you selected the *worst* choice rather than the *best* choice, etc.

3) If the examination is of the objective or multiple-choice type – that is, each question will also give a series of possible answers: A, B, C or D, and you are called upon to select the best answer and write the letter next to that answer on your answer paper – it is advisable to start answering each question in turn. There may be anywhere from 50 to 100 such questions in the three or four hours allotted and you can see how much time would be taken if you read through all the questions before beginning to answer any. Furthermore, if you come across a question or group of questions which you know would be difficult to answer, it would undoubtedly affect your handling of all the other questions.

4) If the examination is of the essay type and contains but a few questions, it is a moot point as to whether you should read all the questions before starting to answer any one. Of course, if you are given a choice – say five out of seven and the like – then it is essential to read all the questions so you can eliminate the two that are most difficult. If, however, you are asked to answer all the questions, there may be danger in trying to answer the easiest one first because you may find that you will spend too much time on it. The best technique is to answer the first question, then proceed to the second, etc.

5) Time your answers. Before the exam begins, write down the time it started, then add the time allowed for the examination and write down the time it must be completed, then divide the time available somewhat as follows:

- If 3-1/2 hours are allowed, that would be 210 minutes. If you have 80 objective-type questions, that would be an average of 2-1/2 minutes per question. Allow yourself no more than 2 minutes per question, or a total of 160 minutes, which will permit about 50 minutes to review.
- If for the time allotment of 210 minutes there are 7 essay questions to answer, that would average about 30 minutes a question. Give yourself only 25 minutes per question so that you have about 35 minutes to review.

6) The most important instruction is to *read each question* and make sure you know what is wanted. The second most important instruction is to *time yourself properly* so that you answer every question. The third most important instruction is to *answer every question*. Guess if you have to but include something for each question. Remember that you will receive no credit for a blank and will probably receive some credit if you write something in answer to an essay question. If you guess a letter – say "B" for a multiple-choice question – you may have guessed right. If you leave a blank as an answer to a multiple-choice question, the examiners may respect your feelings but it will not add a point to your score. Some exams may penalize you for wrong answers, so in such cases *only*, you may not want to guess unless you have some basis for your answer.

7) Suggestions
   a. Objective-type questions
      1. Examine the question booklet for proper sequence of pages and questions
      2. Read all instructions carefully
      3. Skip any question which seems too difficult; return to it after all other questions have been answered
      4. Apportion your time properly; do not spend too much time on any single question or group of questions
      5. Note and underline key words – *all, most, fewest, least, best, worst, same, opposite,* etc.
      6. ~~Pay particular attention to negatives~~
      7. Note unusual option, e.g., unduly long, short, complex, different or similar in content to the body of the question
      8. Observe the use of "hedging" words – *probably, may, most likely,* etc.
      9. Make sure that your answer is put next to the same number as the question
      10. Do not second-guess unless you have good reason to believe the second answer is definitely more correct
      11. Cross out original answer if you decide another answer is more accurate; do not erase until you are ready to hand your paper in
      12. Answer all questions; guess unless instructed otherwise
      13. Leave time for review

   b. Essay questions
      1. Read each question carefully
      2. Determine exactly what is wanted. Underline key words or phrases.
      3. Decide on outline or paragraph answer

4. Include many different points and elements unless asked to develop any one or two points or elements
5. Show impartiality by giving pros and cons unless directed to select one side only
6. Make and write down any assumptions you find necessary to answer the questions
7. Watch your English, grammar, punctuation and choice of words
8. Time your answers; don't crowd material

8) Answering the essay question

Most essay questions can be answered by framing the specific response around several key words or ideas. Here are a few such key words or ideas:

M's: manpower, materials, methods, money, management
P's: purpose, program, policy, plan, procedure, practice, problems, pitfalls, personnel, public relations
   a. Six basic steps in handling problems:
     1. Preliminary plan and background development
     2. Collect information, data and facts
     3. Analyze and interpret information, data and facts
     4. Analyze and develop solutions as well as make recommendations
     5. Prepare report and sell recommendations
     6. Install recommendations and follow up effectiveness

   b. Pitfalls to avoid
     1. *Taking things for granted* – A statement of the situation does not necessarily imply that each of the elements is necessarily true; for example, a complaint may be invalid and biased so that all that can be taken for granted is that a complaint has been registered
     2. *Considering only one side of a situation* – Wherever possible, indicate several alternatives and then point out the reasons you selected the best one
     3. *Failing to indicate follow up* – Whenever your answer indicates action on your part, make certain that you will take proper follow-up action to see how successful your recommendations, procedures or actions turn out to be
     4. *Taking too long in answering any single question* – Remember to time your answers properly

IX. AFTER THE TEST

Scoring procedures differ in detail among civil service jurisdictions although the general principles are the same. Whether the papers are hand-scored or graded by machine we have described, they are nearly always graded by number. That is, the person who marks the paper knows only the number – never the name – of the applicant. Not until all the papers have been graded will they be matched with names. If other tests, such as training and experience or oral interview ratings have been given, scores will be combined. Different parts of the examination usually have different weights. For example, the written test might count 60 percent of the final grade, and a rating of training and experience 40 percent. In many jurisdictions, veterans will have a certain number of points added to their grades.

After the final grade has been determined, the names are placed in grade order and an eligible list is established. There are various methods for resolving ties between those who get the same final grade – probably the most common is to place first the name of the person whose application was received first. Job offers are made from the eligible list in the order the names appear on it. You will be notified of your grade and your rank as soon as all these computations have been made. This will be done as rapidly as possible.

People who are found to meet the requirements in the announcement are called "eligibles." Their names are put on a list of eligible candidates. An eligible's chances of getting a job depend on how high he stands on this list and how fast agencies are filling jobs from the list.

When a job is to be filled from a list of eligibles, the agency asks for the names of people on the list of eligibles for that job. When the civil service commission receives this request, it sends to the agency the names of the three people highest on this list. Or, if the job to be filled has specialized requirements, the office sends the agency the names of the top three persons who meet these requirements from the general list.

The appointing officer makes a choice from among the three people whose names were sent to him. If the selected person accepts the appointment, the names of the others are put back on the list to be considered for future openings.

That is the rule in hiring from all kinds of eligible lists, whether they are for typist, carpenter, chemist, or something else. For every vacancy, the appointing officer has his choice of any one of the top three eligibles on the list. This explains why the person whose name is on top of the list sometimes does not get an appointment when some of the persons lower on the list do. If the appointing officer chooses the second or third eligible, the No. 1 eligible does not get a job at once, but stays on the list until he is appointed or the list is terminated.

X. HOW TO PASS THE INTERVIEW TEST

The examination for which you applied requires an oral interview test. You have already taken the written test and you are now being called for the interview test – the final part of the formal examination.

You may think that it is not possible to prepare for an interview test and that there are no procedures to follow during an interview. Our purpose is to point out some things you can do in advance that will help you and some good rules to follow and pitfalls to avoid while you are being interviewed.

What is an interview supposed to test?

The written examination is designed to test the technical knowledge and competence of the candidate; the oral is designed to evaluate intangible qualities, not readily measured otherwise, and to establish a list showing the relative fitness of each candidate – as measured against his competitors – for the position sought. Scoring is not on the basis of "right" and "wrong," but on a sliding scale of values ranging from "not passable" to "outstanding." As a matter of fact, it is possible to achieve a relatively low score without a single "incorrect" answer because of evident weakness in the qualities being measured.

Occasionally, an examination may consist entirely of an oral test – either an individual or a group oral. In such cases, information is sought concerning the technical knowledges and abilities of the candidate, since there has been no written examination for this purpose. More commonly, however, an oral test is used to supplement a written examination.

Who conducts interviews?

The composition of oral boards varies among different jurisdictions. In nearly all, a representative of the personnel department serves as chairman. One of the members of the board may be a representative of the department in which the candidate would work. In some cases, "outside experts" are used, and, frequently, a businessman or some other representative of the general public is asked to serve. Labor and management or other special groups may be represented. The aim is to secure the services of experts in the appropriate field.

However the board is composed, it is a good idea (and not at all improper or unethical) to ascertain in advance of the interview who the members are and what groups they represent. When you are introduced to them, you will have some idea of their backgrounds and interests, and at least you will not stutter and stammer over their names.

What should be done before the interview?

While knowledge about the board members is useful and takes some of the surprise element out of the interview, there is other preparation which is more substantive. It *is* possible to prepare for an oral interview – in several ways:

1) Keep a copy of your application and review it carefully before the interview

This may be the only document before the oral board, and the starting point of the interview. Know what education and experience you have listed there, and the sequence and dates of all of it. Sometimes the board will ask you to review the highlights of your experience for them; you should not have to hem and haw doing it.

2) Study the class specification and the examination announcement

Usually, the oral board has one or both of these to guide them. The qualities, characteristics or knowledges required by the position sought are stated in these documents. They offer valuable clues as to the nature of the oral interview. For example, if the job involves supervisory responsibilities, the announcement will usually indicate that knowledge of modern supervisory methods and the qualifications of the candidate as a supervisor will be tested. If so, you can expect such questions, frequently in the form of a hypothetical situation which you are expected to solve. NEVER go into an oral without knowledge of the duties and responsibilities of the job you seek.

3) Think through each qualification required

Try to visualize the kind of questions you would ask if you were a board member. How well could you answer them? Try especially to appraise your own knowledge and background in each area, *measured against the job sought,* and identify any areas in which you are weak. Be critical and realistic – do not flatter yourself.

4) Do some general reading in areas in which you feel you may be weak

For example, if the job involves supervision and your past experience has NOT, some general reading in supervisory methods and practices, particularly in the field of human relations, might be useful. Do NOT study agency procedures or detailed manuals. The oral board will be testing your understanding and capacity, not your memory.

5) Get a good night's sleep and watch your general health and mental attitude

You will want a clear head at the interview. Take care of a cold or any other minor ailment, and of course, no hangovers.

What should be done on the day of the interview?

Now comes the day of the interview itself. Give yourself plenty of time to get there. Plan to arrive somewhat ahead of the scheduled time, particularly if your appointment is in the fore part of the day. If a previous candidate fails to appear, the board might be ready for you a bit early. By early afternoon an oral board is almost invariably behind schedule if there are many candidates, and you may have to wait. Take along a book or magazine to read, or your application to review, but leave any extraneous material in the waiting room when you go in for your interview. In any event, relax and compose yourself.

The matter of dress is important. The board is forming impressions about you – from your experience, your manners, your attitude, and your appearance. Give your personal appearance careful attention. Dress your best, but not your flashiest. Choose conservative, appropriate clothing, and be sure it is immaculate. This is a business interview, and your appearance should indicate that you regard it as such. Besides, being well groomed and properly dressed will help boost your confidence.

Sooner or later, someone will call your name and escort you into the interview room. *This is it.* From here on you are on your own. It is too late for any more preparation. But remember, you asked for this opportunity to prove your fitness, and you are here because your request was granted.

What happens when you go in?

The usual sequence of events will be as follows: The clerk (who is often the board stenographer) will introduce you to the chairman of the oral board, who will introduce you to the other members of the board. Acknowledge the introductions before you sit down. Do not be surprised if you find a microphone facing you or a stenotypist sitting by. Oral interviews are usually recorded in the event of an appeal or other review.

Usually the chairman of the board will open the interview by reviewing the highlights of your education and work experience from your application – primarily for the benefit of the other members of the board, as well as to get the material into the record. Do not interrupt or comment unless there is an error or significant misinterpretation; if that is the case, do not hesitate. But do not quibble about insignificant matters. Also, he will usually ask you some question about your education, experience or your present job – partly to get you to start talking and to establish the interviewing "rapport." He may start the actual questioning, or turn it over to one of the other members. Frequently, each member undertakes the questioning on a particular area, one in which he is perhaps most competent, so you can expect each member to participate in the examination. Because time is limited, you may also expect some rather abrupt switches in the direction the questioning takes, so do not be upset by it. Normally, a board member will not pursue a single line of questioning unless he discovers a particular strength or weakness.

After each member has participated, the chairman will usually ask whether any member has any further questions, then will ask you if you have anything you wish to add. Unless you are expecting this question, it may floor you. Worse, it may start you off on an extended, extemporaneous speech. The board is not usually seeking more information. The question is principally to offer you a last opportunity to present further qualifications or to indicate that you have nothing to add. So, if you feel that a significant qualification or characteristic has been overlooked, it is proper to point it out in a sentence or so. Do not compliment the board on the thoroughness of their examination – they have been sketchy, and you know it. If you wish, merely say, "No thank you, I have nothing further to add." This is a point where you can "talk yourself out" of a good impression or fail to present an important bit of information. Remember, *you close the interview yourself.*

The chairman will then say, "That is all, Mr. _____, thank you." Do not be startled; the interview is over, and quicker than you think. Thank him, gather your belongings and take your leave. Save your sigh of relief for the other side of the door.

How to put your best foot forward

Throughout this entire process, you may feel that the board individually and collectively is trying to pierce your defenses, seek out your hidden weaknesses and embarrass and confuse you. Actually, this is not true. They are obliged to make an appraisal of your qualifications for the job you are seeking, and they want to see you in your best light. Remember, they must interview all candidates and a non-cooperative candidate may become a failure in spite of their best efforts to bring out his qualifications. Here are 15 suggestions that will help you:

1) Be natural – Keep your attitude confident, not cocky

If you are not confident that you can do the job, do not expect the board to be. Do not apologize for your weaknesses, try to bring out your strong points. The board is interested in a positive, not negative, presentation. Cockiness will antagonize any board member and make him wonder if you are covering up a weakness by a false show of strength.

2) Get comfortable, but don't lounge or sprawl

Sit erectly but not stiffly. A careless posture may lead the board to conclude that you are careless in other things, or at least that you are not impressed by the importance of the occasion. Either conclusion is natural, even if incorrect. Do not fuss with your clothing, a pencil or an ashtray. Your hands may occasionally be useful to emphasize a point; do not let them become a point of distraction.

3) Do not wisecrack or make small talk

This is a serious situation, and your attitude should show that you consider it as such. Further, the time of the board is limited – they do not want to waste it, and neither should you.

4) Do not exaggerate your experience or abilities

In the first place, from information in the application or other interviews and sources, the board may know more about you than you think. Secondly, you probably will not get away with it. An experienced board is rather adept at spotting such a situation, so do not take the chance.

5) If you know a board member, do not make a point of it, yet do not hide it

Certainly you are not fooling him, and probably not the other members of the board. Do not try to take advantage of your acquaintanceship – it will probably do you little good.

6) Do not dominate the interview

Let the board do that. They will give you the clues – do not assume that you have to do all the talking. Realize that the board has a number of questions to ask you, and do not try to take up all the interview time by showing off your extensive knowledge of the answer to the first one.

7) Be attentive

You only have 20 minutes or so, and you should keep your attention at its sharpest throughout. When a member is addressing a problem or question to you, give him your undivided attention. Address your reply principally to him, but do not exclude the other board members.

8) Do not interrupt

A board member may be stating a problem for you to analyze. He will ask you a question when the time comes. Let him state the problem, and wait for the question.

9) Make sure you understand the question

Do not try to answer until you are sure what the question is. If it is not clear, restate it in your own words or ask the board member to clarify it for you. However, do not haggle about minor elements.

10) Reply promptly but not hastily

A common entry on oral board rating sheets is "candidate responded readily," or "candidate hesitated in replies." Respond as promptly and quickly as you can, but do not jump to a hasty, ill-considered answer.

11) Do not be peremptory in your answers

A brief answer is proper – but do not fire your answer back. That is a losing game from your point of view. The board member can probably ask questions much faster than you can answer them.

12) Do not try to create the answer you think the board member wants

He is interested in what kind of mind you have and how it works – not in playing games. Furthermore, he can usually spot this practice and will actually grade you down on it.

13) Do not switch sides in your reply merely to agree with a board member

Frequently, a member will take a contrary position merely to draw you out and to see if you are willing and able to defend your point of view. Do not start a debate, yet do not surrender a good position. If a position is worth taking, it is worth defending.

14) Do not be afraid to admit an error in judgment if you are shown to be wrong

The board knows that you are forced to reply without any opportunity for careful consideration. Your answer may be demonstrably wrong. If so, admit it and get on with the interview.

15) Do not dwell at length on your present job

The opening question may relate to your present assignment. Answer the question but do not go into an extended discussion. You are being examined for a *new* job, not your present one. As a matter of fact, try to phrase ALL your answers in terms of the job for which you are being examined.

Basis of Rating

Probably you will forget most of these "do's" and "don'ts" when you walk into the oral interview room. Even remembering them all will not ensure you a passing grade. Perhaps you did not have the qualifications in the first place. But remembering them will help you to put your best foot forward, without treading on the toes of the board members.

Rumor and popular opinion to the contrary notwithstanding, an oral board wants you to make the best appearance possible. They know you are under pressure – but they also want to see how you respond to it as a guide to what your reaction would be under the pressures of the job you seek. They will be influenced by the degree of poise you display, the personal traits you show and the manner in which you respond.

ABOUT THIS BOOK

This book contains tests divided into Examination Sections. Go through each test, answering every question in the margin. At the end of each test look at the answer key and check your answers. On the ones you got wrong, look at the right answer choice and learn. Do not fill in the answers first. Do not memorize the questions and answers, but understand the answer and principles involved. On your test, the questions will likely be different from the samples. Questions are changed and new ones added. If you understand these past questions you should have success with any changes that arise. Tests may consist of several types of questions. We have additional books on each subject should more study be advisable or necessary for you. Finally, the more you study, the better prepared you will be. This book is intended to be the last thing you study before you walk into the examination room. Prior study of relevant texts is also recommended. NLC publishes some of these in our Fundamental Series. Knowledge and good sense are important factors in passing your exam. Good luck also helps. So now study this Passbook, absorb the material contained within and take that knowledge into the examination. Then do your best to pass that exam.

EXAMINATION SECTION

EXAMINATION SECTION
TEST 1

DIRECTIONS: Each question or incomplete statement is followed by several suggested answers or completions. Select the one that BEST answers the question or completes the statement. *PRINT THE LETTER OF THE CORRECT ANSWER IN THE SPACE AT THE RIGHT.*

1. The seal of a trap is made of   1._____

   A. a bronze gate   B. a bronze ball
   C. water   D. air

2. When a plumber is using a turnpin, he SHOULD be   2._____

   A. removing kinks from a lead bend
   B. cleaning a lead joint for wiping
   C. straightening out a piece of lead pipe
   D. flaring the end of a lead pipe

3. A water meter measures and registers water consumption in   3._____

   A. gallons per minute   B. cubic feet per hour
   C. quarts per second   D. cubic feet

4. The part that is connected to a ballcock that insures a full trap seal is the   4._____

   A. float ball   B. upper liftrod
   C. hush tube   D. refill tube

5. PROPER protection against excessive pressure within a hot water storage tank is pro-   5._____
   vided by installing a _____ valve.

   A. pressure relief   B. check
   C. flow   D. gate

6. A one-sixteenth bend is EQUIVALENT to a fitting having an angle of _____ degrees.   6._____

   A. 22 1/2   B. 30   C. 45   D. 60

7. A 3-inch standard weight water pipe and a 3-inch extra heavy water pipe have the SAME   7._____

   A. I.D.   B. O.D.
   C. wall thickness   D. weight per foot

8. Of the following materials, the one that is NOT used in caulking a cast iron bell and spigot   8._____
   water pipe joint is

   A. asbestos rope   B. oakum rope
   C. treated paper rope   D. molded rings

9. The reason a cast iron hub is hit before joining the hub with a spigot is to determine its   9._____

   A. soundness   B. weight
   C. wall thickness   D. material content

10. The inside diameter of a 4" brass caulking ferrule is MOST NEARLY   10.____

     A.   3 7/8"   B.   4"   C.   4 1/8"   D.   4 1/4"

11. Cast brass floor flanges used for water closets should have a MINIMUM thickness of   11.____

     A.   1/2"   B.   3/8"   C.   1/4"   D.   1/8"

12. The trap of a water closet is located   12.____

     A.   in the water closet   B.   in the lead bend
     C.   under the water closet   D.   in the soil stack

13. Of the following, a PROPER reason why a plumber should install a check valve is to   13.____

     A.   relieve pressure in the storage tank
     B.   prevent a backflow of sewer gas
     C.   allow a flow of water in one direction only
     D.   reduce the volume of water in an appliance

14. The PURPOSE of an air chamber in a water line is to   14.____

     A.   allow for expansion of water
     B.   increase water pressure in the riser
     C.   reduce water hammer in the system
     D.   decrease velocity of the flow of water

15. As used by a plumber, a leader is a   15.____

     A.   section of a soil stack
     B.   vertical storm water pipe line
     C.   part of a bath waste
     D.   part of a croton

16. The bib-screw in a faucet retains the   16.____

     A.   seat   B.   handle
     C.   washer   D.   packing nut

17. When testing for leaks in gas lines, it is BEST to use   17.____

     A.   water in the lines under pressure
     B.   a lighted candle
     C.   an aquastat
     D.   soapy water

18. Drain lines receiving the discharge from chemistry laboratory sinks should be made of   18.____

     A.   galvanized steel   B.   duriron or pyrex
     C.   cast iron   D.   brass or copper

19. Of the following, the one that is BEST to use when testing for leaks in a new gas pipe installation is a   19.____

     A.   geiger counter   B.   vacuum gauge
     C.   mercury column   D.   water column

20. A plumber should know that installing a globe valve on a cold water line will cut down the _____ of the water.   20.____

    A. volume   B. temperature
    C. viscosity   D. resistance

21. Of the following tools, the one which is NOT used when working a wiped joint is the   21.____

    A. drift plug   B. bending iron
    C. reamer   D. turnpin

22. The amount of lead to be used to complete a caulked cast iron soil joint should NOT be less than _____ of the diameter of the pipe.   22.____

    A. 10 ounces for each inch
    B. 12 ounces for each inch
    C. 14 ounces for each inch
    D. one full medium-sized ladle regardless

23. A shave hook is recommended by its manufacturer for   23.____

    A. evening the edges of lead
    B. brightening oxidized copper
    C. removing burrs from non-ferrous pipe
    D. removing oxidation from lead

24. The MAIN purpose of a house trap is to   24.____

    A. provide the house drain with a cleanout
    B. prevent gases from the public sewer from entering the house plumbing system
    C. *trap* articles of value that are lost
    D. eliminate the necessity for traps under all other fixtures

25. A corporation cock or stop is a   25.____

    A. self-closing faucet
    B. shut-off valve for a lavoratory
    C. frost-proof type of hydrant
    D. shut-off valve for a water service

26. A 45-degree offset included in a house drain should contain ONLY   26.____

    A. one 1/4 bend and one 1/16 bend
    B. one 1/4 bend and one 1/8 bend
    C. two 1/8 bends
    D. two 1/4 bends

27. A plumber prevents siphonage in a fixture trap if he   27.____

    A. vents properly
    B. installs a relief valve
    C. installs the correct number of check valves
    D. provides adequate pitch on the water lines

28. A 28 ft. long pipe line, stalled with a pitch of 1/4 inch per foot, has a TOTAL fall of _____ inches.

    A. 3 1/4   B. 7   C. 10 1/2   D. 14

28.____

29. The length of a pipe measuring 37.875 inches, end-to-end, is EQUAL to 3 ft. + _____ inches.

    A. 0 7/8   B. 1 1/4   C. 1 5/8   D. 1 7/8

29.____

30. A waste stack may receive the discharge from _____ water closet(s).

    A. no   B. only one
    C. two   D. three or more

30.____

31. Capillary action is used in the CORRECT joining of _____ joints.

    A. bell and spigot   B. screw-pipe
    C. copper-tube sweat   D. lead-wiped

31.____

32. The TOTAL length of four pieces of I 1/2" galvanized steel pipe whose lengths are 7 ft. + 3 1/2 inches, 4 f t. + 2 1/4 inches, 6 ft. +7 inches, and 8 ft. + 5 1/8 inches, is _____ ft. + _____ inches.

    A. 26; 5 7/8   B. 25; 6 7/8
    C. 25; 4 1/4   D. 25; 3 3/8

32.____

33. To a plumber, the letters I.P.S. mean

    A. internal pipe size
    B. iron pipe size
    C. interior pressure standards
    D. international pipe standard.

33.____

34. Of the following, the tool that SHOULD be used on polished pipe surface is the

    A. Stillson wrench   B. strap wrench
    C. chain tongs   D. crescent wrench

34.____

35. In plumbing, the abbreviation X.H.C.I. is associated with

    A. water heaters   B. chemical waste lines
    C. air lines   D. house drains

35.____

36. A yarning iron SHOULD be used in

    A. tinning copper fittings
    B. making lead safes
    C. making bell and spigot joints
    D. drying a water-filled trench

36.____

37. If a 45-degree offset is 12 inches in length, the length of its diagonal or travel is _____ inches.

    A. 17   B. 18   C. 19   D. 20

37.____

38. *Plumbers Soil* is GENERALLY used by plumbers as an aid in   38.____

    A. wiping lead joints   B. making up flange joints
    C. backfilling a trench   D. threading steel pipes

39. Of the following types of saws, the one that SHOULD be used for cutting lead pipe is the   39.____
    _____ saw.

    A. cross-cut   B. rip
    C. hack   D. dove-tail

40. Of the following fixtures, the one that plumbers USUALLY call the *unit fixture* is the   40.____

    A. water closet   B. slop sink
    C. lavatory   D. bathtub

KEY (CORRECT ANSWERS)

1. C	11. D	21. C	31. C
2. D	12. A	22. B	32. A
3. D	13. C	23. D	33. B
4. D	14. C	24. B	34. B
5. A	15. B	25. D	35. D
6. A	16. C	26. C	36. C
7. B	17. D	27. A	37. A
8. B	18. B	28. B	38. A
9. A	19. C	29. D	39. A
10. D	20. A	30. A	40. C

TEST 2

DIRECTIONS: Each question or incomplete statement is followed by several suggested answers or completions. Select the one that BEST answers the question or completes the statement. *PRINT THE LETTER OF THE CORRECT ANSWER IN THE SPACE AT THE RIGHT.*

1. The vertical distance between the crown weir and the dip of a trap is called the   1.____

    A. jumpover   B. air gap
    C. seal depth   D. diameter of the trap

2. Of the following, the composition of general purpose *wiping solder* is _____ tin and _____ lead.   2.____

    A. 70%; 30%   B. 60%; 40%   C. 50%; 50%   D. 35%; 65%

3. Of the following wrenches, the one which should be used on screwed valves and fittings having hexagonal connections is the _____ wrench.   3.____

    A. pipe   B. monkey   C. chuck   D. strap

4. A cast iron coupling that has one end threaded for screw pipe and the other end hubbed to receive the spigot end of a pipe is known as a(n)   4.____

    A. sisson fitting   B. tucker fitting
    C. union   D. F & W fitting

5. The size of a fresh-air inlet is based on the size of the associated   5.____

    A. house drain   B. public sewer
    C. house sewer   D. soil stack

6. The tool that holds the dies when pipe is being threaded is called a   6.____

    A. yoke   B. vise   C. stock   D. swedge

7. A gallon of water weighs MOST NEARLY _____ lbs.   7.____

    A. 6.25   B. 7.5   C. 8.33   D. 14.7

8. A *solder nipple* is MAINLY used in plumbing work to   8.____

    A. maintain an even flow of solder
    B. connect the handle of a soldering iron to the *copper*
    C. make up a joint between lead pipe and brass pipe
    D. clean clogged pipes

9. Where steel hangers are used to support copper pipe, the pipe should be insulated from the hangers to prevent   9.____

    A. water hammer   B. vibration
    C. cooling   D. electrolysis

10. Copper tubing having the GREATEST wall thickness is known as _____ copper tubing.   10.____

    A. D.W.V. type   B. type M
    C. type L   D. type K

11. Of the following methods, the BEST one to use in making up a pipe joint between lead pipe and copper pipe is

    A. brazing   B. soldering
    C. burning   D. wiping

11.____

12. To *break in* or condition a new asbestos joint runner, the runner SHOULD be soaked in

    A. alcohol   B. rosin   C. oil   D. water

12.____

13. The weight of a 4 ft. x 4 ft. shower pan made of 6-pound lead is MOST NEARLY _____ pounds.

    A. 96   B. 75   C. 69   D. 29.25

13.____

14. The approved method of making a branch connection to an existing horizontal cast iron wasteline is by using a

    A. sisson fitting   B. kaeffer fitting
    C. saddle   D. three-piece connection

14.____

15. A *hydropneumatic* tank in a plumbing system is MAINLY used to

    A. pump storm water to the sewer
    B. provide potable water under pressure
    C. supply compressed air to equipment
    D. filter water for a swimming pool.

15.____

16. Syphon action through the fill pipe in a flush tank is prevented by installing a

    A. stop and waste valve   B. vacuum breaker
    C. flushometer   D. back-water valve

16.____

17. Sperm candle or tallon is applied to clean lead work in order to PREVENT

    A. pitting   B. oxidation
    C. tinning   D. melting

17.____

18. Joints for cast iron bell and spigot soil pipe SHOULD be made with

    A. wiped solder
    B. packed oakum and molten lead
    C. oakum and asphaltic compound
    D. oakum and cement mortar

18.____

19. A tee whose branch is larger than the run is CORRECTLY referred to as a _____ tee.

    A. bullhead   B. lateral   C. street   D. reducing

19.____

20. A house drain which is buried in earth SHOULD be made of

    A. galvanized wrought iron   B. galvanized steel
    C. transite   D. uncoated cast iron

20.____

21. A compression type fitting is MOST frequently used with

    A. copper tubing   B. steel pipe
    C. transite   D. cast iron pipe

21.____

22. Safety goggles should be worn when cutting 22._____

    A. galvanized pipe   B. oakum
    C. cast iron   D. sheet lead

23. A plumber should NOT plunge a wet ladle into a pot of molten caulking lead because it 23._____

    A. contaminates the lead   B. may crack the pot
    C. may crack the ladle   D. makes the lead spatter

24. A plumber's helper who is careless is one who is 24._____

    A. negligent   B. untrained
    C. neat   D. methodical

25. A CORRECTLY installed gasket provides a seal in a 25._____

    A. flange union   B. ground joint union
    C. roof flange   D. left-right coupling

26. A plumber installing a battery of sinks in the kitchen of a school cafeteria should also include in the waste line a(n) 26._____

    A. chlorinator   B. anti-syphon loop
    C. grease trap   D. check valve

27. If a faucet continues to drip despite the new washer a helper has installed, he SHOULD then 27._____

    A. reface or replace the seat
    B. install a washer made of different material
    C. replace the entire faucet
    D. replace the bib-screw

28. Of the following tools, the one used to fasten faucets to lavatories is called a(n) 28._____

    A. pair of pump pliers   B. spud wrench
    C. open-end wrench   D. basin wrench

29. A cast iron floor flange SHOULD be used when installing a 29._____

    A. water closet   B. bathtub
    C. kitchen sink   D. drinking fountain

30. A plumber's rasp is a tool recommended by its manufacturer for use on 30._____

    A. cast iron   B. brass
    C. lead   D. black steel

31. Of the following, the pipe size NOT common to the plumbing trade is _____ inch. 31._____

    A. 2   B. 2 1/2   C. 3   D. 3 1/2

32. Once a flushometer valve is in operation, it is made to close automatically by the 32._____

    A. return of the lever handle to the neutral position
    B. action of a flat helical spring above the diaphragm
    C. water pressure on the inlet side of the valve
    D. elasticity of a stainless steel diaphragm

Questions 33-36.

DIRECTIONS: Questions 33 through 36, inclusive, are to be answered by referring to the following sketch of a piping arrangement.

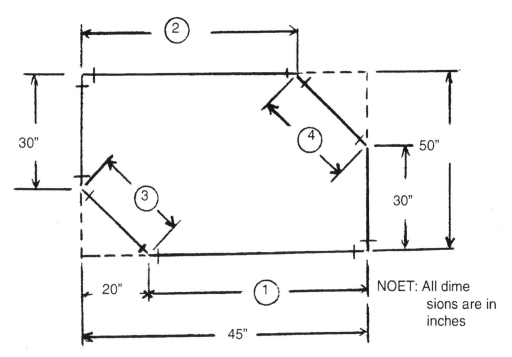

NOET: All dime
sions are in
inches

33. The center-to-center pipe measurement of *1* is MOST NEARLY equal to _____ inches.   33.____

A. 20   B. 25   C. 30   D. 65

34. The center-to-center pipe measurement of *2* is MOST NEARLY equal to _____ inches.   34.____

A. 20   B. 25   C. 30   D. 45

35. The center-to-center pipe measurement of *3* is MOST NEARLY equal to _____ inches.   35.____

A. 30 1/2   B. 28 7/8   C. 28 1/4   D. 27 3/4

36. The center-to-center pipe measurement of *4* is MOST NEARLY equal to _____ inches.   36.____

A. 23 1/2   B. 28 1/4   C. 29   D. 31 1/4

37. An outside caulking iron is a tool recommended by its manufacturer for use on   37.____

A. steel pipe   B. cast iron
C. lead pipe   D. brass pipe

38. A swimming pool is 25 feet wide by 75 feet long and has an average depth of 5 feet.   38.____
The capacity when filled to the overflow is _____ gallons.

A. 9,375   B. 65,625   C. 69,005   D. 70,312

39. A tap borer SHOULD be used by a plumber when 39._____

    A. cutting internal threads
    B. preparing copper joints for sweating
    C. joining cast iron to screw pipe
    D. preparing soil lead pipe for a solder nipple

40. A hydrostatic test on a plumbing system SHOULD be done by using 40._____

    A. water   B. smoke   C. air   D. kerosene

_____

KEY (CORRECT ANSWERS)

1. C	11. D	21. A	31. D
2. D	12. C	22. C	32. C
3. B	13. A	23. D	33. B
4. B	14. D	24. A	34. B
5. A	15. B	25. A	35. C
6. C	16. B	26. C	36. B
7. C	17. B	27. A	37. B
8. C	18. B	28. D	38. D
9. D	19. A	29. A	39. D
10. D	20. D	30. C	40. A

_____

EXAMINATION SECTION
TEST 1

DIRECTIONS: Each question or incomplete statement is followed by several suggested answers or completions. Select the one that BEST answers the question or completes the statement. *PRINT THE LETTER OF THE CORRECT ANSWER IN THE SPACE AT THE RIGHT.*

1. The combustion efficiency of a boiler can be determined with a CO_2 indicator and the

    A. under fire draft   B. boiler room humidity
    C. flue gas temperature   D. outside air temperature

1.____

2. A quick, practical method of determining if the cast-iron waste pipe delivered to a job has been damaged in transit is to

    A. hydraulically test it
    B. "ring" each length with a hammer
    C. drop each length to see whether it breaks
    D. visually examine the pipe for cracks

2.____

3. An electrostatic precipitator is used to

    A. filter the air supply
    B. remove sludge from the fuel oil
    C. remove particles from the fuel gas
    D. supply samples for an Orsat analysis

3.____

4. The PRIMARY cause of cracking and spalling of refractory lining in the furnace of a steam generator is *most likely* due to

    A. continuous over-firing of boiler
    B. slag accumulation on furnace walls
    C. change in fuel from solid to liquid
    D. uneven heating and cooling within the refractory brick

4.____

5. The term "effective temperature" in air conditioning means

    A. the dry bulb temperature
    B. the average of the wet and dry bulb temperatures
    C. the square root of the product of wet and dry bulb temperatures
    D. an arbitrary index combining the effects of temperature, humidity, and movement

5.____

6. The piping in all buildings having dual water distribution systems should be identified by a color coding of _____ for potable water lines and _____ for non-potable water lines.

    A. green; red   B. green; yellow
    C. yellow; green   D. yellow; red

6.____

7. The breaking of a component of a machine subjected to excessive vibration is called

    A. tensile failure   B. fatigue failure
    C. caustic embrittlement   D. amplitude failure

7.____

8. The TWO MOST important factors to be considered in selecting fans for ventilating systems are 8.____

   A. noise and efficiency
   B. space available and weight
   C. first cost and dimensional bulk
   D. construction and arrangement of drive

9. In the modern power plant deaerator, air is removed from water to 9.____

   A. reduce heat losses in the heaters
   B. reduce corrosion of boiler steel due to the air
   C. reduce the load of the main condenser air pumps
   D. prevent pumps from becoming vapor bound

10. The abbreviations BOD, COD, and DO are associated with 10.____

   A. flue gas analysis   B. air pollution control
   C. boiler water treatment   D. water pollution control

11. The piping of a newly installed drainage system should be tested upon completion of the rough plumbing with a head of water of NOT LESS THAN _____ feet. 11.____

   A. 10   B. 15   C. 20   D. 25

12. Of the following statements concerning aquastats, the one which is CORRECT is: 12.____

   A. Aquastats may be obtained with either a narrow or wide range of settings
   B. Aquastats have a mercury tube switch which is controlled by the stack switch
   C. An aquastat is a device used to shut down the burner in the event of low water in the boiler
   D. An aquastat should be located about 4 inches above the normal water line of the boiler

13. The SAFEST way to protect the domestic water supply from contamination by sewage or non-potable water is to insert 13.____

   A. air gaps
   B. swing connections
   C. double check valves
   D. tanks with overhead discharge

14. The MAIN function of a back-pressure valve which is sometimes found in the connection between a water drain pipe and the sewer system is to 14.____

   A. equalize the pressure between the drain pipe and the sewer
   B. prevent sewer water from flowing into the drain pipe
   C. provide pressure to enable waste to reach the sewer
   D. make sure that there is not too much water pressure in the sewer line

15. Boiler water is neutral if its pH value is 15.____

   A. 0   B. 1   C. 7   D. 14

16. A domestic hot water mixing or tempering valve should be preceded in the hot water line   16.____
    by a

    A. strainer   B. foot valve
    C. check valve   D. steam trap

17. Between a steam boiler and its safety valve there should be   17.____

    A. no valve of any type
    B. a gate valve of the same size as the safety valve
    C. a swing check valve of at least the same size as the safety valve
    D. a cock having a clear opening equal in area to the pipe connecting the boiler and
        safety valve

18. A diagram of horizontal plumbing drainage lines should have cleanouts shown   18.____

    A. at least every 25 feet
    B. at least every 100 feet
    C. wherever a basin is located
    D. wherever a change in direction occurs

19. When a Bourdon gauge is used to measure steam pressures, some form of siphon or   19.____
    water seal must be maintained.
    The reason for this is to

    A. obtain "absolute" pressure readings
    B. prevent steam from entering the gage
    C. prevent condensate from entering the gage
    D. obtain readings below atmospheric pressure

20. In a closed heat exchanger, oil is cooled by condensate which is to be returned to a   20.____
    boiler. In order to avoid the possibility of contaminating the condensate with oil should a
    tube fail in the oil cooler, it would be good practice to

    A. cool the oil by air instead of water
    B. treat the condensate with an oil solvent
    C. keep the oil pressure in the exchanger higher than the water pressure
    D. keep the water pressure in the exchanger higher than the oil pressure

21. A radiator thermostatic trap is used on a vacuum return type of heating system to   21.____

    A. release the pocketed air only
    B. reduce the amount of condensate
    C. maintain a predetermined radiator water level
    D. prevent the return of live steam to the return line

22. According to the color coding of piping, fire protection piping should be painted   22.____

    A. green   B. yellow   C. purple   D. red

23. The MAIN purpose of a standpipe system is to   23.____

    A. supply the roof water tank
    B. provide water for firefighting

C. circulate water for the heating system
D. provide adequate pressure for the water supply

24. The name "Saybolt" is associated with the measurement of   24.____

    A. viscosity   B. Btu content
    C. octane rating   D. temperature

25. Recirculation of conditioned air in an air-conditioned building is done MAINLY to   25.____

    A. reduce refrigeration tonnage required
    B. increase room entrophy
    C. increase air specific humidity
    D. reduce room temperature below the dewpoint

26. In a plumbing installation, vent pipes are GENERALLY used to   26.____

    A. prevent the loss of water seal from traps by evaporation
    B. prevent the loss of water seal due to several causes other than evaporation
    C. act as an additional path for liquids to flow through during normal use of a plumb-
       ing fixture
    D. prevent the backflow of water in a cross-connection between a drinking water line
       and a sewage line

27. The designation "150 W" cast on the bonnet of a gate valve is an indication of the   27.____

    A. water working temperature
    B. water working pressure
    C. area of the opening in square inches
    D. weight of the valve in pounds

28. In the city, the size soil pipe necessary in a sewage drainage system is determined by   28.____
    the

    A. legal occupancy of the building
    B. vertical height of the soil line
    C. number of restrooms connected to the soil line
    D. number of "fixture units" connected to the soil line

29. Fins or other extended surfaces are used on heat exchanger tubes when   29.____

    A. the exchanger is a water-to-water exchanger
    B. water is on one side of the tube and condensing steam on the other side
    C. the surface coefficient of heat transfer on both sides of the tube is high
    D. the surface coefficient of heat transfer on one side of the tube is low compared to
       the coefficient on the other side of the tube

30. A fusible plug may be put in a fire tube boiler as an emergency device to indicate low   30.____
    water level. The fusible plug is installed so that under normal operating conditions,

    A. both sides are exposed to steam
    B. one side is exposed to water and the other side to steam
    C. one side is exposed to steam and the other side to hot gases
    D. one side is exposed to the water and the other side to hot gases

31. Extra strong wrought-iron pipe, as compared to standard wrought-iron pipe of the same nominal size, has   31._____

    A.   the same outside diameter but a smaller inside diameter
    B.   the same inside diameter but a larger outside diameter
    C.   a larger outside diameter and a smaller inside diameter
    D.   larger inside and outside diameters

32. Fans may be rated on a dynamic or a static efficiency basis. The dynamic efficiency would *probably* be   32._____

    A.   lower in value because of the energy absorbed by the air velocity
    B.   the same as the static in the case of centrifugal blowers running at various speeds
    C.   the same as the static in the case of axial flow blowers running at various speeds
    D.   higher in value than the static

33. The function of the stack relay in an oil burner installation is to   33._____

    A.   regulate the draft over the fire
    B.   regulate the flow of fuel oil to the burner
    C.   stop the motor if the oil has not ignited
    D.   stop the motor if the water or steam pressure is too high

34. The type of centrifugal pump which is inherently balanced for hydraulic thrust is the   34._____

    A.   double suction impeller type
    B.   single suction impeller type
    C.   single stage type
    D.   multistage type

35. The specifications for a job using sheet lead calls for "4-lb. sheet lead." This means that each sheet should weigh   35._____

    A.   4 lbs.   B.   4 lbs. per square
    C.   4 lbs. per square foot   D.   4 lbs. per cubic inch

36. The total cooling load design conditions for a building are divided for convenience into two components.
These are: 36._____

    A.   infiltration and radiation
    B.   sensible heat and latent heat
    C.   wet and dry bulb temperatures
    D.   solar heat gain and moisture transfer

37. The function of a Hartford loop used on some steam boilers is to   37._____

    A.   limit boiler steam pressure
    B.   limit temperature of the steam
    C.   prevent high water levels in the boiler
    D.   prevent back flow of water from the boiler into the return main

38. Vibration from a ventilating blower can be prevented from being transmitted to the duct   38.____
work by

    A.   installing straighteners in the duct
    B.   throttling the air supply to the blower
    C.   bolting the blower tightly to the duct
    D.   installing a canvas sleeve at the blower outlet

39. A specification states that access panels to suspended ceiling will be of metal.   39.____
The MAIN reason for providing access panels is to

    A.   improve the insulation of the ceiling
    B.   improve the appearance of the ceiling
    C.   make it easier to construct the building
    D.   make it easier to maintain the building

40. A plumber on a job reports that the steamfitter has installed a 3" steam line in a location   40.____
at which the plans show the house trap. On inspecting the job,
you should

    A.   tell the steamfitter to remove the steam line
    B.   study the condition to see if the house trap can be relocated
    C.   tell the plumber and steamfitter to work it out between themselves and then report
to you
    D.   tell the plumber to find another location for the trap because the steamfitter has
already completed his work

41. In the installation of any heating system, the MOST important consideration is that   41.____

    A.   all elements be made of a good grade of cast iron
    B.   all radiators and connectors be mounted horizontally
    C.   the smallest velocity of flow of heating medium be used
    D.   there be proper clearance between hot surfaces and surrounding combustible
material

42. Which one of the following is the PRIMARY object in drawing up a set of specifications   42.____
for materials to be purchased?

    A.   Control of quality
    B.   Outline of intended use
    C.   Establishment of standard sizes
    D.   Location and method of inspection.

43. The drawing which should be used as a LEGAL reference when checking completed   43.____
construction work is the _____ drawing.

    A.   contract   B.   assembly
    C.   working or shop   D.   preliminary

Questions 44-50.

DIRECTIONS: Questions 44 through 50 refer to the plumbing drawing shown below.

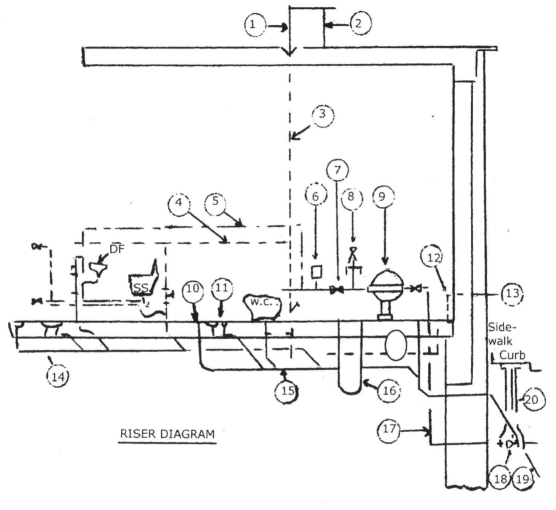

RISER DIAGRAM

44. According to the building code, the MINIMUM diameter of No. (1) and its minimum   44._____

    height, No. (2) respectively, are

    A. 2" and 12"   B. 3" and 18"
    C. 4" and 24"   D. 6" and 36"

45. No (6) is a   45._____

    A. relief valve   B. shock absorber
    C. testing connection   D. drain

46. No. (9) is a   46._____

    A. strainer   B. float valve
    C. meter   D. pedestal

47. No. (11) is a   47._____

    A. floor drain   B. cleanout
    C. trap   D. vent connection

48. No. (13) is a   48.___

    A. standpipe   B. air inlet
    C. sprinkler head   D. cleanout

49. The size of No. (16) is   49.___

    A. 2" x 2"   B. 2" x 3"
    C. 3" x 3"   D. 4" x 4"

50. No. (18) is a   50.___

    A. pressure reducing valve
    B. butterfly valve
    C. curb cock
    D. sprinkler head

KEY (CORRECT ANSWERS)

No.	Ans	No.	Ans	No.	Ans	No.	Ans	No.	Ans
1.	C	11.	A	21.	D	31.	A	41.	D
2.	B	12.	C	22.	D	32.	D	42.	A
3.	C	13.	A	23.	B	33.	C	43.	A
4.	D	14.	B	24.	A	34.	A	44.	C
5.	D	15.	C	25.	A	35.	C	45.	B
6.	B	16.	A	26.	B	36.	B	46.	C
7.	B	17.	A	27.	B	37.	D	47.	A
8.	A	18.	D	28.	D	38.	D	48.	B
9.	B	19.	B	29.	D	39.	D	49.	D
10.	D	20.	D	30.	D	40.	B	50.	C

EXAMINATION SECTION
TEST 1

DIRECTIONS: Each question or incomplete statement is followed by several suggested answers or completions. Select the one that BEST answers the question or completes the statement. *PRINT THE LETTER OF THE CORRECT ANSWER IN THE SPACE AT THE RIGHT.*

1. The function of a trap in a plumbing line is to prevent

    A. water hammer
    B. cross connections
    C. sewer gases from backing up
    D. leakage from a connection

1.____

2. The term *roughing in* means installing

    A. the vent lines
    B. all plumbing except the fixtures
    C. the drain pipes
    D. the soil lines

2.____

3. An expansion bolt is used to

    A. enlarge a hole
    B. fasten into hollow tile
    C. allow for expansion and contraction
    D. fasten into solid masonry

3.____

4. The purpose of the smoke test is to

    A. detect defects in plumbing installations
    B. check the operation of the boiler
    C. analyze flue gases
    D. test fire-retarding materials

4.____

5. Of the following traps, the one which is NORMALLY used to retain steam in a heating unit or piping is the _____ trap.

    A. P   B. running   C. float   D. bell

5.____

6. Of the following materials, the one which is a convenient and powerful adhesive for cementing tears in canvas jackets that are wrapped around warm pipe insulation is

    A. cylinder oil   B. wheat paste
    C. water glass   D. latex paint

6.____

7. Pipe chases should be provided with an access door PRIMARILY to provide means to

    A. replace piping lines
    B. either inspect or manipulate valves
    C. prevent condensate from forming on the pipes
    D. check the chase for possible structural defects

7.____

8. To remove a stoppage in a trap which has not cleared by use of a force cup, the tool to use is a(n)

    A. yarning tool   B. auger
    C. expansion bit   D. trowel

8._____

9. If the float of a flush tank leaks and fills with water, the MOST probable result will be

    A. no water in the tank
    B. ball cock will remain open
    C. water will flow over tank rim onto floor
    D. flush ball will not seat properly

9._____

10. Which of the following valves does NOT have a wheel and stem?

    A. Globe   B. Gate   C. Check   D. Plug cock

10._____

11. If a radiator is air-bound, the MOST likely cause is

    A. no condensate return
    B. defective steam valve
    C. defective air valve
    D. too much air carried in steam

11._____

12. When color marking is used, potable water lines are painted

    A. yellow   B. blue   C. red   D. green

12._____

13. A set of mechanical plan drawings is drawn to a scale of 1/8" = 1 foot.
If a length of pipe measures 15 7/16" on the drawing, the ACTUAL length of the pipe is _____ feet.

    A. 121.5   B. 122.5   C. 123.5   D. 124.5

13._____

14. Packing is used in an adjustable water valve MAINLY to

    A. make it air-tight
    B. prevent mechanical wear
    C. regulate the water pressure
    D. make it water-tight

14._____

15. Good practice requires that the end of a piece of water pipe be reamed to remove the inside burr after it has been cut to length.
The purpose of the reaming is to

    A. finish the pipe accurately to length
    B. make the threading easier
    C. avoid cutting of the workers' hands
    D. allow free passage for the flow of water

15._____

16. The BEST wrench to use to tighten a galvanized iron pipe valve or fitting which has hexagonal ends is a _____ wrench.

    A. stillson   B. strap   C. monkey   D. socket

16._____

17. A flushometer would be connected to a

    A. water meter   B. toilet bowl
    C. garden hose   D. fire hose

17._____

18. The purpose of a chase is to

    A. support an elbow
    B. accommodate pipes in a wall
    C. accommodate flashing in a parapet
    D. provide venting

18._____

19. Refrigeration piping, valves, fittings, and related parts used in the construction and installation of refrigeration systems shall conform to the

    A. American Society of Mechanical Engineers Boiler and Pressure Vessel Code
    B. American Standards Association Code for Pressure Piping
    C. Pipe Fabrication Institute Standards
    D. Underwriters Laboratory Standards

19._____

20. For pipe sizes up to 8", schedule 40 pipe is identical to _____ pipe.

    A. standard   B. extra strong
    C. double extra strong   D. type M copper

20._____

21. A metallic underground water piping system is to be used as a means of grounding. Of the following statements concerning use of this system, the one that is MOST NEARLY CORRECT is that this use is

    A. not permitted
    B. permitted where available
    C. absolutely required
    D. permitted only in certain cases

21._____

22. On a piping plan drawing, the symbol shown at the right represents a 90° _____ elbow.
    A. flanged
    B. screwed
    C. bell and spigot
    D. welded

22._____

23. Of the following piping materials, the one that combines the physical strength of mild steel with the corrosion resistance of gray iron is

    A. grade A steel   B. grey cast iron
    C. welded wrought iron   D. ductile iron

23._____

24. Of the following uses, the one for which a bituminous compound would USUALLY be used is to

    A. prevent corrosion of burled steel tanks
    B. increase the strength of concrete
    C. caulk water pipes
    D. paint inside wood columns

24._____

25. In accordance with established jurisdictional work procedures among the trades, the person you would assign to replace a malfunctioning fire sprinkler head would be a   25.____

    A. plumber
    C. housesmith
    B. laborer
    D. steamfitter

KEY (CORRECT ANSWERS)

1. C		11. C	
2. B		12. D	
3. D		13. C	
4. A		14. D	
5. C		15. D	
6. C		16. C	
7. B		17. B	
8. B		18. B	
9. B		19. B	
10. C		20. A	

21.	B
22.	A
23.	D
24.	A
25.	D

TEST 2

DIRECTIONS: Each question or incomplete statement is followed by several suggested answers or completions. Select the one that BEST answers the question or completes the statement. *PRINT THE LETTER OF THE CORRECT ANSWER IN THE SPACE AT THE RIGHT.*

1. The MOST likely reason for a cold water faucet to continue to drip after its washer has been replaced is a defective

    A. handle   B. stem   C. seat   D. bib

    1.____

2. In water lines, the type of valve which should ALWAYS be either fully open or fully closed is the _____ valve.

    A. needle   B. gate   C. globe   D. mixing

    2.____

3. The BEST tool to use on a 1" galvanized iron pipe nipple when unscrewing the nipple from a coupling is a _____ wrench.

    A. crescent   B. stillson   C. monkey   D. spud

    3.____

4. The BEST way to locate a leak in a natural gas pipe line is to

    A. hold a lighted match under the pipe and move it along the length of the pipe slowly
    B. hold a lighted match about two inches above the pipe and move it along the length of the pipe slowly
    C. coat the pipe with a soapy solution and watch for bubbles
    D. shut off the gas at the meter and then coat the pipe with a soapy solution and watch for bubbles

    4.____

5. The brownish discoloration that sometimes occurs in a hot water circulating system is USUALLY due to

    A. molds   B. algae   C. bacteria   D. rust

    5.____

6. The type of valve that does NOT have a stuffing or packing gland is a _____ valve.

    A. globe   B. radiator   C. check   D. gate

    6.____

7. Assuming that the hot and cold water demand of a fixture will be the same, then the normal size of the hot water pipe with respect to that of the cold water pipe should be

    A. the same
    B. twice as great
    C. one and one-half times as great
    D. one-half as great

    7.____

8. If the pitch of a horizontal steam line is 1/2 inch in 10 feet, one end of a 45-foot steam line is lower than the other end by MOST NEARLY _____ inches.

    A. 2   B. 2 1/4   C. 3   D. 3 1/2

    8.____

9. A pump that removes 30 gallons of water per minute is pumping water from a cellar 30 feet x 50 feet covered with eight inches of water. One cubic foot of water equals 7.5 gallons of water.
The number of minutes it will take to remove the eight inches of water from the cellar is MOST NEARLY

    A. 200   B. 225   C. 250   D. 275

9.____

10. The pipe fitting required for connecting the 1 inch pipe to the one and a half inch valve is a
    A. close nipple
    B. street ell
    C. reducing bushing
    D. reducing coupling

10.____

$1\frac{1}{2}"$ VALVE

1" PIPE

11. Compression fittings are MOST often used with

    A. cast iron bell and spigot pipe
    B. steel flange pipe
    C. copper tubing
    D. transite

11.____

12. Water hammer is BEST eliminated by

    A. increasing the size of all the piping
    B. installing an air chamber
    C. replacing the valve seats with neoprene gaskets
    D. flushing the system to remove corrosion

12.____

13. The BEST type of pipe to use in a gas line in a domestic installation is

    A. black iron   B. galvanized iron
    C. cast iron   D. wrought steel

13.____

14. If there is a pinhole in the float of a toilet tank, the

    A. water will flush continuously
    B. toilet cannot flush
    C. tank cannot be filled with water
    D. valve will not shut off so water will overflow into the overflow tube

14.____

15. Condensation of moisture in humid weather occurs MOST often on _____ pipe(s).

    A. sewage   B. gas
    C. hot water   D. cold water

15.____

16. A gas appliance should be connected to a gas line by means of a(n)

    A. union   B. right and left coupling
    C. elbow   D. close nipple

16.____

17. A PRINCIPAL difference between a pipe thread and a machine thread is that the pipe thread is   17.____

    A. tapered   B. finer   C. flat   D. longer

18. When joining galvanized iron pipe, pipe joint compound is placed on   18.____

    A. the female threads only
    B. the male threads only
    C. both the male and female threads
    D. either the male or female threads, depending on the type of fitting

19. The U-bend in the sink drain pipe is MAINLY for the purpose of preventing   19.____
    A. water leakage
    B. waste back-up
    C. hammer noise in the pipe
    D. back-up of foul air

Questions 20-21.

DIRECTIONS: Questions 20 and 21 are to be answered on the basis of the following paragraph.

For cast iron pipe lines, the middle ring or sleeve shall have beveled ends and shall be high quality cast iron. The middle ring shall have a minimum wall thickness of 3/8" for pipe up to 8", 7/16" for pipe 10" to 30", and 1/2" for pipe over 30", nominal diameter. Minimum length of middle ring shall be 5" for pipe up to 10", 6" for pipe 10" to 30", and 10" for pipe 30" nominal diameter and larger. The middle ring shall not have a center pipe stop, unless otherwise specified.

20. As used in the above paragraph, the word *beveled* means MOST NEARLY   20.____

    A. straight   B. slanted   C. curved   D. rounded

21. In accordance with the above paragraph, the middle ring of a 24" nominal diameter pipe would have a MINIMUM wall thickness and length of _____ thick and _____ long.   21.____

    A. 3/8"; 5"   B. 3/8"; 6"   C. 7/16"; 6"   D. 1/2"; 6"

22. A gland bushing is associated in practice with a(n)   22.____

    A. gas engine   B. electric motor
    C. centrifugal pump   D. lathe

23. A house drain is successively offset by means of a 1/8 bend, a 1/16 bend, and a 1/32   23.___
    bend.
    The total angular offset of this line is MOST NEARLY

    A. 34⁰   B. 39⁰   C. 68⁰   D. 79⁰

24. The flushing mechanism in a low tank water closet is so arranged that a fill tube supplies   24.___
    water from the ball cock to the overflow stand pipe for a short interval immediately after
    the closet is flushed.
    The MAIN reason for this is to

    A. finish cleaning the water passages of the closet
    B. properly seal the ball in its seat
    C. renew the seal in the closet trap
    D. scour the flush tube from the tank to the closet

25. A small pump impeller is checked for static balance by   25.___

    A. running the pump at high speed and listening for rubs
    B. mounting it on parallel and level knife edges and noting if it turns
    C. weighing it and comparing the weight against the original weight
    D. putting it on a lathe to see if it runs true

KEY (CORRECT ANSWERS)

1. C	11. C		
2. B	12. B		
3. B	13. A		
4. C	14. D		
5. D	15. D		
6. C	16. B		
7. A	17. A		
8. B	18. B		
9. C	19. D		
10. C	20. B		

21. C
22. C
23. D
24. C
25. B

TEST 3

DIRECTIONS: Each question or incomplete statement is followed by several suggested answers or completions. Select the one that BEST answers the question or completes the statement. *PRINT THE LETTER OF THE CORRECT ANSWER IN THE SPACE AT THE RIGHT.*

1. Back-pressure valves are provided in the connections between drain pipes and the sewer system to

    A. equalize drain pipe and sewer pressure
    B. insure water flow from the sewer to the drain pipe
    C. prevent water from the sewer system from going into the drain pipe
    D. provide pressure to enable the water to flow in either direction

1.____

2. A non-rising steam type gate valve is ESPECIALLY useful where

    A. the stem must move downward only
    B. the pressure in the pipe must remain constant
    C. clearances around the valve are limited
    D. hand control of the valve is not required

2.____

3. Ferrules or sleeves in the walls and roof of the subway structure are provided for

    A. insulating the structure from the ground
    B. water pipes which pass through the structure
    C. reinforcing the concrete
    D. cooling the concrete while it is setting

3.____

4. Hair felt is commonly used for

    A. heat insulation   B. electrical insulation
    C. grouting   D. reinforcement

4.____

5. When making up a pipe joint in the shop, between a nipple and a valve, the

    A. valve should be held in a square-jawed vise and the pipe screwed into it
    B. pipe should be held in a square-jawed vise and the valve screwed onto it
    C. valve should be held in a pipe vise and the pipe screwed into it
    D. pipe should be held in a pipe vise and the valve screwed onto it

5.____

6. A water meter is USUALLY read in

    A. pounds   B. cubic feet
    C. pounds per square inch   D. degrees

6.____

7. The valve which AUTOMATICALLY prevents back flow in a water pipe is called a _____ valve.

    A. check   B. globe   C. gate   D. by-pass

7.____

8. A motor driven centrifugal pump takes water from a main and delivers it to the nozzles of a train washing machine. With little change in motor speed or suction pressure, the discharge pressure rises and the flow of cleaning water falls to a trickle.
The PROBABLE cause is a

8.____

A. failure of the impeller shaft
B. leak in the piping between the pressure gage point of attachment and the nozzles
C. blockage of the impeller
D. blockage between the pressure gage point of attachment and the nozzles

9. The term *bell and spigot* USUALLY refers to   9.___

    A. refrigerator motors   B. cast iron pipes
    C. steam radiator outlets   D. electrical receptacles

10. In plumbing work, a valve which allows water to flow in one direction only is commonly   10.___
known as a _____ valve.

    A. check   B. globe   C. gate   D. stop

11. A pipe coupling is BEST used to connect two pieces of pipe of   11.___

    A. the same diameter in a straight line
    B. the same diameter at right angles to each other
    C. different diameters at a 45° angle
    D. different diameters at an1/8th bend

12. A fitting or pipe with many outlets relatively close together is commonly called a   12.___

    A. manifold   B. gooseneck
    C. flange union   D. return bend

13. To locate the center in the end of a sound shaft, the BEST tool to use is a(n)   13.___

    A. ruler   B. divider
    C. hermaphrodite caliper   D. micrometer

14. When cutting a piece of 1 1/4" O.D. 20 gauge brass tubing with a hand hacksaw, it is   14.___
BEST to use a blade having _____ teeth per inch.

    A. 14   B. 18   C. 22   D. 32

15. When cutting a piece of 1"' O.D. extra-heavy pipe with a pipe cutter, a burr usually forms   15.___
on the inside and the outside of the pipe.
These burrs are BEST removed by means of a pipe

    A. tap and a file   B. wrench and rough stone
    C. reamer and a file   D. drill and a chisel

16. In making up the piping shown at the right,
one piece of pipe was cut the wrong length
so that the union at location *A* would not
meet as shown.
The pipe which was cut wrong MUST have
been pipe number
    A. 1
    B. 2
    C. 3
    D. 4

17. Of the following piping, the one that CANNOT be termed a stack is _____ piping. 17.____

    A. soil   B. house drain
    C. vent   D. waste

18. A pipe coupling is a plumbing fitting that is MOST commonly used to join 18.____

    A. two pieces of threaded pipe of the same diameter
    B. a large diameter tubing to a smaller diameter threaded pipe
    C. two pieces of threaded pipe of different diameters
    D. a large diameter threaded pipe to a smaller diameter tubing

19. Of the following, the MOST important reason for replacing a worn washer in a dripping 19.____
faucet as soon as possible is to prevent

    A. overflow of the sink tap
    B. the mixture of hot and cold water in the sink
    C. damage to the faucet parts that can be the result of overtightening the stem
    D. air from entering the supply line

20. A wiped joint is MOST likely to be found in _____ piping. 20.____

    A. vitrified clay sewer   B. cast iron sewer
    C. steel water   D. lead

21. A caulked joint is MOST likely to be found in 21.____

    A. vitrified clay sewer piping
    B. bell and spigot metal piping
    C. brass water piping
    D. a connection between a brass pipe and a lead pipe

22. Of the following materials, the one that the city building code does NOT permit for use in 22.____
underground piping is _____ pipe.

    A. wrought iron   B. cast iron
    C. lead   D. brass

23. The drainage system of a building is that part of the plumbing system which receives, 23.____
conveys, and removes

    A. the discharge of any fixture except water closets
    B. storm water only
    C. liquid and water carried wastes and storm water
    D. the discharge of water closets only

24. GENERALLY, water supply pipes running outside a subway structure which are located 24.____
less than four feet below a street are covered with insulating material to protect them
from

    A. street heat   B. high voltage
    C. freezing   D. vibration

25. Multiple threads are used on the stems of some large valves to   25.____

    A. reduce the effort required to open the valve
    B. prevent binding of the valve stem
    C. secure faster opening and closing of the valve
    D. decrease the length of stem travel

KEY (CORRECT ANSWERS)

1.	C		11.	A
2.	C		12.	A
3.	B		13.	C
4.	A		14.	D
5.	D		15.	C
6.	B		16.	C
7.	A		17.	B
8.	D		18.	A
9.	B		19.	C
10.	A		20.	D

21.	B
22.	A
23.	C
24.	C
25.	C

ARITHMETICAL REASONING
EXAMINATION SECTION
TEST 1

DIRECTIONS: Each question or incomplete statement is followed by several suggested answers or completions. Select the one that BEST answers the question or completes the statement. *PRINT THE LETTER OF THE CORRECT ANSWER IN THE SPACE AT THE RIGHT.*

1.   1.____

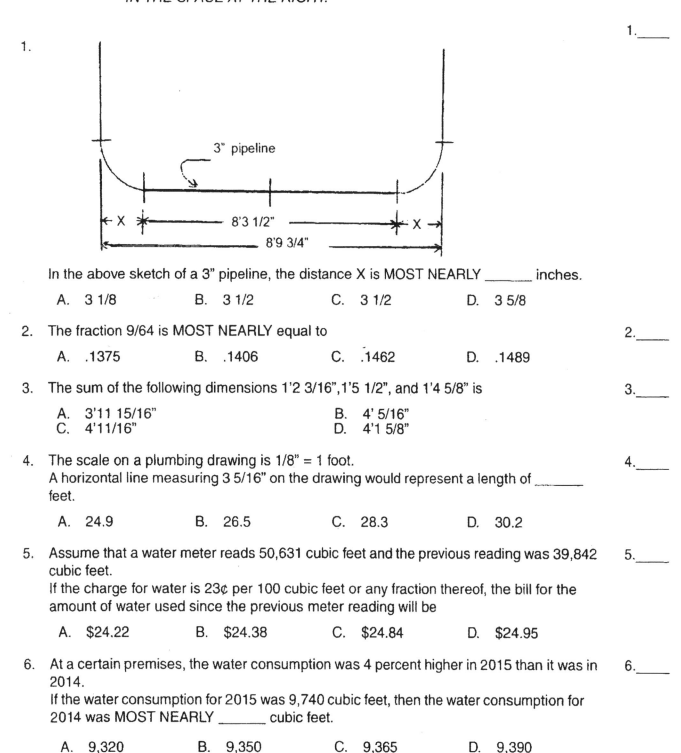

In the above sketch of a 3" pipeline, the distance X is MOST NEARLY _____ inches.

   A. 3 1/8   B. 3 1/2   C. 3 1/2   D. 3 5/8

2. The fraction 9/64 is MOST NEARLY equal to   2.____

   A. .1375   B. .1406   C. .1462   D. .1489

3. The sum of the following dimensions 1'2 3/16",1'5 1/2", and 1'4 5/8" is   3.____

   A. 3'11 15/16"   B. 4' 5/16"
   C. 4'11/16"   D. 4'1 5/8"

4. The scale on a plumbing drawing is 1/8" = 1 foot.   4.____
A horizontal line measuring 3 5/16" on the drawing would represent a length of _____ feet.

   A. 24.9   B. 26.5   C. 28.3   D. 30.2

5. Assume that a water meter reads 50,631 cubic feet and the previous reading was 39,842 cubic feet.   5.____
If the charge for water is 23¢ per 100 cubic feet or any fraction thereof, the bill for the amount of water used since the previous meter reading will be

   A. $24.22   B. $24.38   C. $24.84   D. $24.95

6. At a certain premises, the water consumption was 4 percent higher in 2015 than it was in 2014.   6.____
If the water consumption for 2015 was 9,740 cubic feet, then the water consumption for 2014 was MOST NEARLY _____ cubic feet.

   A. 9,320   B. 9,350   C. 9,365   D. 9,390

7. A pump delivers water at a constant rate of 40 gallons per minute.   7.____
   If there are 7.5 gallons to a cubic foot of water, the time it will take to fill a tank 6 feet x
   5 feet x 4 feet is MOST NEARLY _____ minutes.

    A. 15   B. 22.5   C. 28.5   D. 30

8. The total weight, in pounds, of three lengths of 3" cast-iron pipe 7'6" long, weighing 14.5   8.____
   pounds per foot, and four lengths of 4" cast-iron pipe each 5'0" long, weighing 13.0
   pounds per foot, is MOST NEARLY

    A. 540   B. 585   C. 600   D. 665

9. The water pressure at the bottom of a column of water 34 feet high is 14.7 lbs./sq.in.   9.____
   The water pressure in lbs./sq.in. at the bottom of the column of water 12 feet high is
   MOST NEARLY

    A. 3   B. 5   C. 7   D. 9

10. The number of cubic yards of earth that would be removed when digging a trench 8 feet   10.____
    wide x 9 feet deep x 63 feet long is

    A. 56   B. 168   C. 314   D. 504

11. On test, a meter registered one cubic foot for each 1 1/3 cubic feet of water that passed   11.____
    through it.
    If the meter had a reading of 1,200 cubic feet, we may conclude that the CORRECT
    amount should be _____ cubic feet.

    A. 800   B. 900   C. 1,500   D. 1,600

12. A water use meter reads 87,463 cubic feet.   12.____
    If the previous reading was 17,377 cubic feet and the rate charged is 15 cents per 100
    cubic feet, the bill for water use during this period is about

    A. $45.00   B. $65.00   C. $85.00   D. $105.00

13. Under proper conditions, the one of the following groups of pipes that gives the same   13.____
    flow in gals/min as one 6" diameter pipe is (neglect friction) _____ pipes of _____
    diameter each.

    A. 3; 3"   B. 4; 3"   C. 2; 4"   D. 3; 4"

14. A roof tank is used to furnish the domestic water supply to a ten story building. This tank   14.____
    has a capacity of 5,900 gallons. At 10:00 A.M. one morning, the tank is half full.
    If water is being used at the rate of 50 gals/min, the pump which is used to fill the tank
    has a rated capacity of 90 gals/min, the time it would take to fill the tank
    under these conditions is MOST NEARLY _____ hour(s),
    _____ minutes.

    A. 2; 8   B. 1; 14   C. 2; 32   D. 1; 2

15. The number of gallons of water contained in a cylindrical swimming pool 8 feet in diame-   15.____
    ter and filled to a depth of 3 feet 6 inches is MOST NEARLY (assume 7.5 gallons = 1
    cubic foot)

    A. 30   B. 225   C. 1,320   D. 3,000

16. The charge for metered water is 52 1/2 cents per hundred cubic feet, with a minimum charge of $21 per annum. Of the following, the SMALLEST water usage in hundred cubic feet that would result in a charge GREATER than the minimum is   16.____

    A. 39   B. 40   C. 41   D. 42

17. The annual frontage rent on a one-story building 40 ft. in length is $735.00. For each additional story, $52.50 per annum is added to the frontage rent. For demolition, the charge for wetting down is 3/8 of the annual frontage charge.   17.____
The charge for wetting down a building six stories in height, with a 40 ft. frontage, is MOST NEARLY

    A. $369   B. $371   C. $372   D. $374

18. If the drawing of a piping layout is made to a scale of 1/4" equals one foot, then a 7'9" length of piping would be represented by a scaled length on the drawing of APPROXI-MATELY _____ inches.   18.____

    A. 2   B. 7 3/4   C. 23 1/4   D. 31

19. A plumbing sketch is drawn to a scale of eighth-size. A line measuring 3" on the sketch would be equivalent to _____ feet.   19.____

    A. 2   B. 6   C. 12   D. 24

20. If 500 feet of pipe weighs 800 lbs., the number of pounds that 120 feet will weigh is MOST NEARLY   20.____

    A. 190   B. 210   C. 230   D. 240

21. If a trench is excavated 3'0" wide by 5'6" deep and 50 feet long, the total number of cubic yards of earth removed is MOST NEARLY   21.____

    A. 30   B. 90   C. 150   D. 825

22. Assume that a plumber earns $86,500 per year.   22.____
If eighteen percent of his pay is deducted for taxes and social security, his net weekly pay will be APPROXIMATELY

    A. $1,326   B. $1,365   C. $1,436   D. $1,457.50

23. Assume that a plumbing installation is made up of the following fixtures and groups of fix-tures: 12 bathroom groups each containing one W.C., one lavatory, and one bathtub with shower; 12 bathroom groups each containing one W.C., one lavatory, one bathtub, and one shower stall; 24 combination kitchen fixtures; 4 floor drains; 6 slop sinks without flushing rim; and 2 shower stalls (or shower bath).   23.____
The total number of fixtures for the above plumbing installation is MOST NEARLY

    A. 60   B. 95   C. 120   D. 210

24. A triangular opening in a wall forms a 30-60 degree right triangle.   24.____
If the longest side measures 12'0", then the shortest side will measure

    A. 3'0"   B. 4'0"   C. 6'0"   D. 8'0"

25. You are directed to cut 4 pieces of pipe, one each of the following length: 2'6 1/4",
3'9 3/8", 4'7 5/8", and 5'8 7/8".
The total length of these 4 pieces is

   A. 15'7 1/4"   B. 15'9 3/8"   C. 16'5 7/8"   D. 16'8 1/8"

25.____

KEY (CORRECT ANSWERS)

1.	A	11.	D
2.	B	12.	D
3.	B	13.	B
4.	B	14.	B
5.	C	15.	C
6.	C	16.	C
7.	B	17.	D
8.	B	18.	A
9.	B	19.	A
10.	B	20.	A

21.	A
22.	B
23.	C
24.	C
25.	D

SOLUTIONS TO PROBLEMS

1. 8'3 1/2" + x + x = 8'9 3/4" Then, 2x = 6 1/4", so x = 3 1/8"

2. 9/64 = .140625 = .1406

3. 1'2 3/16" + 1'5 1/2" +1'4 5/8" = 3'11 21/16" = 4'5/16"

4. 3 5/16" ÷ 1/8" =53/16 x 8/1 = 26.5. Then, (26.5)(1 ft.) = 26.5 feet

5. 50,631 - 39,842 = 10,789; 10,789 ÷ 100 = 107.89
   Since the cost is .23 per 100 cubic feet or any fraction thereof, the cost will be
   (.23)(107) + .23 = $24.84

6. 9740 ÷ 1.04 = 9365 cu.ft.

7. 40 ÷ 7.5 = 5 1/3 cu.ft. of water per minute. The volume = (6)(5)(4) = 120 cu.ft. Thus, the number of minutes needed to fill the tank is 120 ÷ 5 1/3 = 22.5

8. 3" pipe: 3 x 7'6" = 22 1/2' x 14.5 lbs. = 326.25
   4" pipe: 4 x 5' = 20' x 13 lbs. = 260
   326.25 + 260 = 586.25 (most nearly 585)

9. Let x = pressure. Then, 34/12 = 14.7/x. So, 34x = 176.4
   Solving, x $\approx$ 5 lbs./sq.in.

10. (8)(9)(63) = 4536 cu.ft. Since 1 cu.yd. = 27 cu.ft., 4536 cu.ft. is equivalent to 168 cu.yds.

11. Let x = correct amount. Then, $\dfrac{1}{1200} = \dfrac{1\frac{1}{3}}{x}$. Solving, x = 1600

12. 87,463 - 17,377 = 70,086; and 70,086 ÷ 100 = 700.86 $\approx$ 700 Then, (700)(.15) = $105.00

13. Cross-sectional area of a 6" diameter pipe = $(\pi)(3")^2 = 9\pi$ sq. in. Note that the combined cross-sectional areas of four 3" diameter pipes = $(4)(\pi)(1.5")^2 = 9\pi$ sq . in .

14. 90 - 50 = 40 gals/min. Then, 2950 ÷ 40 = 73.75 min. $\approx$ 1 hr. 14 min.

15. Volume = $(\pi)(4)^2(3\ 1/2) = 56\pi$ cu.ft. Then, $(56\pi)(7.5) = 1320$ gals.

16. For 4100 cu.ft., the charge of (.525)(41) = $21,525 > $21

17. Rent = $73,500 + (5)($52.50) = $997,50. For demolition, the charge = (3/8)($997.50) $374

18. (1/4")(7.75) = 2"

19. (3")(8) = 24" = 2 ft.

20. Let x = weight. Then, 500/800 = 120/x . Solving, x = 192 190 lbs.

21. (3')(5 1/2')(50') = 825 cu.ft. Then, 825 ÷ 27 ≈ 30 cu.yds.

22. Net pay = (.82)($86,500) = $70,930/yr. Weekly pay = $70,930 ÷ 52 ≈ $1365

23. (12x3) + (12x4) +24+4+6+2= 120

24. The shortest side = (1/2)(hypotenuse) = (1/2)(12') = 6'

25. 2'6 1/4" + 3'9 3/8" + 4'7 5/8" + 5'8 7/8 " = 14'30 17/8" = 16'8 1/8"

TEST 2

DIRECTIONS: Each question or incomplete statement is followed by several suggested answers or completions. Select the one that BEST answers the question or completes the statement. *PRINT THE LETTER OF THE CORRECT ANSWER IN THE SPACE AT THE RIGHT.*

1. The sum of the following pipe lengths, 15 5/8", 8 3/4", 30 5/16" and 20 1/2", is   1._____

    A. 77 1/8"   B. 76 3/16"   C. 75 3/16"   D. 74 5/16"

2. If the outside diameter of a pipe is 6 inches and the wall thickness is 1/2 inch, the inside   2._____
area of this pipe, in square inches, is MOST NEARLY

    A. 15.7   B. 17.3   C. 19.6   D. 23.8

3. Three lengths of pipe 1'10", 3'2 1/2", and 5'7 1/2", respectively, are to be cut from a pipe   3._____
14'0" long.
Allowing 1/8" for each pipe cut, the length of pipe remaining is

    A. 3'1 1/8"   B. 3'2 1/2"   C. 3'3 1/4"   D. 3'3 5/8"

4. According to the building code, the MAXIMUM permitted surface temperature of combus-   4._____
tible construction materials located near heating equipment is 76.5°C. ($°F=(°Cx9/5)+32$)
Maximum temperature Fahrenheit is MOST NEARLY

    A. 170° F   B. 195° F   C. 210° F   D. 220° F

5. A pump discharges 7.5 gals/minutes.   5._____
In 2.5 hours the pump will discharge _____ gallons.

    A. 1125   B. 1875   C. 1950   D. 2200

6. A pipe with an outside diameter of 4" has a circumference of MOST NEARLY _____   6._____
inches.

    A. 8.05   B. 9.81   C. 12.57   D. 14.92

7. A piping sketch is drawn to a scale of 1/8" = 1 foot.   7._____
A vertical steam line measuring 3 1/2" on the sketch would have an ACTUAL length of
_____ feet.

    A. 16   B. 22   C. 24   D. 28

8. A pipe having an inside diameter of 3.48 inches and a wall thickness of .18 inches will   8._____
have an outside diameter of _____ inches.

    A. 3.84   B. 3.64   C. 3.57   D. 3.51

9. A rectangular steel bar having a volume of 30 cubic inches, a width of 2 inches, and a   9._____
height of 3 inches will have a length of _____ inches.

    A. 12   B. 10   C. 8   D. 5

10. A pipe weighs 20.4 pounds per foot of length.   10._____
The total weight of eight pieces of this pipe with each piece 20 feet in length is MOST
NEARLY _____ pounds.

    A. 460   B. 1,680   C. 2,420   D. 3,260

11. Assume that four pieces of pipe measuring 2'1 1/4", 4'2 3/4", 5'1 9/16", and 6'3 5/8", respectively, are cut with a saw from a pipe 20"0" long.
Allowing 1/16" waste for each cut, the length of the remaining pipe is   11.___

    A. 2'1 9/16"   B. 2'2 9/16"   C. 2'4 13/16"   D. 2'8 9/16"

12. If one cubic inch of steel weighs 0.28 pounds, the weight, in pounds, of a steel bar 1/2" x 6" x 2'0" long is MOST NEARLY   12.___

    A. 11   B. 16   C. 20   D. 24

13. If the circumference of a circle is equal to 31.416 inches, then its diameter, in inches, is equal to MOST NEARLY   13.___

    A. 8   B. 9   C. 10   D. 13

14. Assume that a steam fitter's helper receives a salary of $171.36 a day for 250 days is considered a full work year. If taxes, social security, hospitalization, and pension deducted from his salary amounts to 16 percent of his gross pay, then his net yearly salary will be MOST NEARLY   14.___

    A. $31,788   B. $35,982   C. $41,982   D. $42,840

15. If the outside diameter of a pipe is 14 inches and the wall thickness is 1/2 inch, then the inside area of the pipe, in square inches, is MOST NEARLY   15.___

    A. 125   B. 133   C. 143   D. 154

16. A steam leak in a pipe line allows steam to escape at a rate of 50,000 pounds each month.
Assuming that the cost of steam is $2.50 per 1,000 pounds, the TOTAL cost of wasted steam from this leak for a 12-month period would amount to   16.___

    A. $125   B. $300   C. $1,500   D. $3,000

17. If 250 feet of 4" pipe weighs 400 pounds, the weight of this pipe per linear foot is _____ pounds.   17.___

    A. 1.25   B. 1.50   C. 1.60   D. 1.75

18. A set of heating plan drawings is drawn to a scale of 1/4" = 1 foot.
If a length of pipe measures 4 5/8" on the drawing, the ACTUAL length of the pipe, in feet, is   18.___

    A. 16.3   B. 16.8   C. 17.5   D. 18.5

19. The TOTAL length of four pieces of pipe whose lengths are 3'4 1/2", 2'1 5/16", 4'9 3/8", and 2'3 1/4", respectively, is   19.___

    A. 11'5 7/16"   B. 11'6 7/16"
    C. 12'5 7/16"   D. 12'6 7/16"

20. Assume that a pipe trench is 3 feet wide, 3 feet deep, and 300 feet long.
If the unit cost of excavating the trench is $120 per cubic yard, the TOTAL cost of excavating the trench is   20.___

    A. $1,200   B. $12,000   C. $27,000   D. $36,000

21. The TOTAL length of four pieces of 1 1/2" galvanized steel pipe whose lengths are 7 ft. + 3 1/2 inches, 4 ft. + 2 1/4 inches, 6 ft. + 7 inches, and 8 ft. +5 1/8 inches is

    21.____

    A. 26 feet + 5 7/8 inches   B. 25 ft. + 6 7/8 inches
    C. 25 feet + 4 1/4 inches   D. 25 ft. + 3 3/8 inches

22. A swimming pool is 25' wide by 75' long and has an average depth of 5'. 1 cubic foot contains 7.5 gallons of water. The capacity, when filled to the overflow, is _____ gallons.

    22.____

    A. 9,375   B. 65,625   C. 69,005   D. 70,312

23. The sum of 3 1/4, 5 1/8, 2 1/2 , and 3 3/8 is

    23.____

    A. 14   B. 14 1/8   C. 14 1/4   D. 14 3/8

24. Assume that it takes 6 men 8 days to do a particular job. If you have only 4 men available to do this job and they all work at the same speed, then the number of days it would take to complete the job would be

    24.____

    A. 11   B. 12   C. 13   D. 14

25. The total length of four pieces of 2" O.D. pipe, whose lengths are 7'3 1/2", 4'2 3/16", 5'7 5/16", and 8'5 7/8", respectively, is MOST NEARLY

    25.____

    A. 24'6 3/4"   B. 24'7 15/16"
    C. 25'5 13/16"   D. 25'6 7/8"

KEY (CORRECT ANSWERS)

1.	C	11.	B
2.	C	12.	C
3.	D	13.	C
4.	A	14.	B
5.	A	15.	B
6.	C	16.	C
7.	D	17.	C
8.	A	18.	D
9.	D	19.	D
10.	D	20.	B

21.	A
22.	D
23.	C
24.	B
25.	D

SOLUTIONS TO PROBLEMS

1. 15 5/8" + 8 3/4" + 30 5/16" + 20 1/2" = 73 35/16" = 75 3/16"

2. Inside diameter = 6" - 1/2" - 1/2" = 5". Area = $(\pi)(5/2")^2 \approx 19.6$ sq. in.

3. Pipe remaining = 14' - 1'10" - 3'2 1/2" - 5'7 1/2" - (3)(1/8") = 3'3 5/8"

4. 76.5 x 9/5 = 137.7 + 32 = 169.7

5. 7.5 x 150 = 1125

6. Radius = 2" Circumference = $(2\pi)(2") \approx 12.57"$

7. 3 1/2" 1/8" = (7/2)(8/1) = 28 Then, (28)(1 ft.) = 28 feet

8. Outside diameter = 3.48" + .18" + .18" = 3.84"

9. 30 = (2)(3)(length). So, length = 5"

10. Total weight = (20.4)(8)(20) $\approx$ 3260 lbs.

11. 20' - 2'1 1/4" - 4'2 3/4" - 5'1 9/16" - 6'3 5/8" - (4)(1/16") = 2'2 9/16"

12. Weight = (.28)(1/2")(6")(24") = 20.16 $\approx$ 20 lbs.

13. Diameter = 31.416" $\div \pi \approx$ 10"

14. His net pay for 250 days = (.84)($171.36)(250) = $35,985.60 $\approx$ $35,928 (from answer key)

15. Inside diameter = 14" - 1/2" - 1/2" = 13". Area = $(\pi)(13/2")^2 \approx$ 133 sq.in

16. (50,000 lbs.)(12) = 600,000 lbs. per year. The cost would be ($2.50)(600) = $1500

17. 400 $\div$ 250 = 1.60 pounds per linear foot

18. 4 5/8" $\div$ 1/4" = 37/8 . 4/1 = 18.5 Then, (18.5)(1 ft.) = 18.5 feet

19. 3'4 1/2" + 2'1 5/16" + 4'9 3/8" + 2'3 1/4" = 11'17 23/16" = 12'6 7/16"

20. (3')(3')(300') = 2700 cu.ft., which is 2700 $\div$ 27 = 100 cu.yds. Total cost = ($120)(100) = $12,000

21. 7'3 1/2" + 4'2 1/4" + 6'7" + 8'5 1/8" = 25'17 7/8" = 26'5 7/8"

22. (25)(75)(5) = 9375 cu.ft. Then, (9375)(7.5) $\approx$ 70,312 gals.

23. 3 1/4 + 5 1/8 + 2 1/2 + 3 3/8 = 13 10/8 = 14 1/4

24. (6) (8) = 48 man-days. Then, 48 $\div$ 4 = 12 days

25. 7'3 1/2" + 4'2 3/16" + 5'7 5/16" + 8'5 7/8"= 24'17 30/16" = 25'6 7/8"

TEST 3

DIRECTIONS: Each question or incomplete statement is followed by several suggested answers or completions. Select the one that BEST answers the question or completes the statement. *PRINT THE LETTER OF THE CORRECT ANSWER IN THE SPACE AT THE RIGHT.*

1. The time required to pump 2,500 gallons of water out of a sump at the rate of 12 1/2 gallons per minutes would be _____ hour(s) _____ minutes.

    A. 1; 40   B. 2; 30   C. 3; 20   D. 6; 40   1.____

2. Copper tubing which has an inside diameter of 1 1/16" and a wall thickness of .095" has an outside diameter which is MOST NEARLY _____ inches.

    A. 1 5/32   B. 1 3/16   C. 1 7/32   D. 1 1/4   2.____

3. Assume that 90 gallons per minute flow through a certain 3-inch pipe which is tapped into a street main.
The amount of water which would flow through a 1-inch pipe tapped into the same street main is MOST NEARLY _____ gpm.

    A. 90   B. 45   C. 30   D. 10   3.____

4. The weight of a 6 foot length of 8-inch pipe which weighs 24.70 pounds per foot is _____ lbs.

    A. 148.2   B. 176.8   C. 197.6   D. 212.4   4.____

5. If a 4-inch pipe is directly coupled to a 2-inch pipe and 16 gallons per minute are flowing through the 4-inch pipe, then the flow through the 2-inch pipe will be _____ gallons per minute.

    A. 4   B. 8   C. 16   D. 32   5.____

6. If the water pressure at the bottom of a column of water 34 feet high is 14.7 pounds per square inch, the water pressure at the bottom of a column of water 18 feet high is MOST NEARLY _____ pounds per square inch.

    A. 8.0   B. 7.8   C. 7.6   D. 7.4   6.____

7. If there are 7 1/2 gallons in a cubic foot of water and if water flows from a hose at a constant rate of 4 gallons per minute, the time it should take to COMPLETELY fill a tank of 1,600 cubic feet capacity with water from that hose is _____ hours.

    A. 300   B. 150   C. 100   D. 50   7.____

8. Each of a group of fifteen water meter readers read an average of 62 water meters a day in a certain 5-day work week. A total of 5,115 meters are read by this group the following week.
The TOTAL number of meters read in the second week as compared to the first week shows a

    A. 10% increase   B. 15% increase   8.____
    C. 20% increase   D. 5% decrease

9. A certain water consumer used 5% more water in 1994 than he did in 1993.
   If his water consumption for 1994 was 8,375 cubic feet, the amount of water he consumed in 1993 was MOST NEARLY _____ cubic feet.

   A. 9,014   B. 8,816   C. 7,976   D. 6,776

      9.___

10. Assume that a water meter reads 40,175 cubic feet and that the previous reading was 29,186 cubic feet.
    If the charge for water is 92 cents per 100 cubic feet or any fraction thereof, the bill for the amount of water used since the previous meter reading should be

    A. $100.28   B. $101.04   C. $101.08   D. $101.20

      10.___

11. A leaking faucet caused a loss of 216 cubic feet of water in a 30-day month.
    If there are 7.5 gallons in a cubic foot of water, then the AVERAGE loss of water per hour for that month was _____ gallons.

    A. 2 1/4   B. 2 1/8   C. 2   D. 1 3/4

      11.___

12. The fraction which is equal to .375 is

    A. 3/16   B. 5/32   C. 3/8   D. 5/12

      12.___

13. A square backyard swimming pool, each side of which is 10 feet long, is filled to a depth of 3 1/2 feet.
    If there are 7 1/2 gallons in a cubic foot of water, the number of gallons of water in the pool is MOST NEARLY _____ gallons.

    A. 46.7   B. 100   C. 2,625   D. 3,500

      13.___

14. When 1 5/8, 3 3/4, 6 1/3, and 9 1/2 are added, the resulting sum is

    A. 21 1/8   B. 21 1/6   C. 21 5/24   D. 21 1/4

      14.___

15. When 946 1/2 is subtracted from 1,035 1/4, the result is

    A. 87 1/4   B. 87 3/4   C. 88 1/4   D. 88 3/4

      15.___

16. When 39 is multiplied by 697, the result is

    A. 8,364   B. 26,283   C. 27,183   D. 28,003

      16.___

17. When 16.074 is divided by .045, the result is

    A. 3.6   B. 35.7   C. 357.2   D. 3,572

      17.___

18. To dig a trench 3'0" wide, 50'0" long, and 5'6" deep, the total number of cubic yards of earth to be removed is MOST NEARLY

    A. 30   B. 90   C. 140   D. 825

      18.___

19. The TOTAL length of four pieces of 2" pipe, whose lengths are 7'3 1/2", 4'2 3/16", 5'7 5/16", and 8'5 7/8", respectively, is

    A. 24'6 3/4"   B. 24'7 15/16"
    C. 25'5 13/16"   D. 25'6 7/8"

      19.___

20. A hot water line made of copper has a straight horizontal run of 150 feet and, when installed, is at a temperature of 45° F. In use, its temperature rises to 190° F.
If the coefficient of expansion for copper is 0.0000095" per foot per degree F, the TOTAL expansion, in inches, in the run of pipe is given by the product of 150 multiplied by 0.0000095 by

20.____

   A. 145
   C. 145 divided by 12
   B. 145 x 12
   D. 145 x 12 x 12

21. A water storage tank measures 5' long, 4' wide, and 6' deep and is filled to the 5 1/2' mark with water.
If one cubic foot of water weighs 62 pounds, the number of pounds of water required to COMPLETELY fill the tank is

21.____

   A. 7,440   B. 6,200   C. 1,240   D. 620

22. Assume that a pipe worker earns $83,125.00 per year.
If seventeen percent of his pay is deducted for taxes, social security, and pension, his net weekly pay will be APPROXIMATELY

22.____

   A. $1598.50   B. $1504.00   C. $1453.00   D. $1325.00

23. If eighteen feet of 4" cast iron pipe weighs approximately 390 pounds, the weight of this pipe per lineal foot will be MOST NEARLY _____ lbs.

23.____

   A. 19   B. 22   C. 23   D. 25

24. If it takes 3 men 11 days to dig a trench, the number of days it will take 5 men to dig the same trench, assuming all work is done at the same rate of speed, is MOST NEARLY

24.____

   A. 6 1/2   B. 7 3/4   C. 8 1/4   D. 8 3/4

25. If a trench is dug 6'0" deep, 2'6" wide, and 8'0" long, the area of the opening, in square feet, is MOST NEARLY

25.____

   A. 48   B. 32   C. 20   D. 15

———

KEY (CORRECT ANSWERS)

1.	C	11.	A
2.	D	12.	C
3.	D	13.	C
4.	A	14.	C
5.	B	15.	D
6.	B	16.	C
7.	D	17.	C
8.	A	18.	A
9.	C	19.	D
10.	D	20.	A

21.	D
22.	D
23.	B
24.	A
25.	C

———

SOLUTIONS TO PROBLEMS

1. 2500 ÷ 12 1/2 = 200 min. = 3 hrs. 20 min.

2. 1 1/16" + .095" + .095" = 1.0625 + .095 + .095 = 1.2525" ≈ 1 1/4"

3. Cross-sectional areas for a 3-inch pipe and a 1-inch pipe are $(\pi)(1.5)^2$ and $(\pi)(.5)^2$ = 2.25 π and .25 π, respectively. Let x = amount of water flowing through the 1-inch pipe. Then, $\frac{90}{x} = \frac{2.25\pi}{.25\pi}$. Solving, x = 10 gals/min

4. (24.70)(6) = 148.2 lbs.

5. $\frac{4" \text{ pipe}}{16 \text{ gallons}} = \frac{2" \text{ pipe}}{x \text{ gallons}}$, 4x = 32, x = 8

6. Let x = pressure. Then, 34/18 = 14.7/x . Solving, x ≈ 7.8

7. (1600)(7.5) = 12,000 gallons. Then, 12,000 ÷ 4 = 3000 min. = 50 hours

8. (15)(62)(5) = 4650. Then, (5115-4650)/4650 = 10% increase

9. 8375 ÷ 1.05 ≈ 7976 cu.ft.

10. 40,175 - 29,186 = 10,989 cu.ft. Then, 10,989 100 = 109.89. Since .92 is charged for each 100 cu.ft. or fraction thereof, total cost = (.92)(110) = $101.20

11. (216)(7.5) = 1620 gallons. In 30 days, there are 720 hours. Thus, the average water loss per hour = 1620 ÷ 720 = 2 1/4 gallons.

12. .375 = 375/1000 = 3/8

13. Volume = (10)(10)(3 1/2) = 350 cu.ft. Then, (350)(7 1/2) = 2625 gallons

14. 1 5/8 + 3 3/4 + 6 1/3 + 9 1/2 = 19 53/24 = 21 5/24

15. 1035 1/4 - 946 1/2 = 88 3/4

16. (39)(697) = 27,183

17. 16.074 .045 = 357.2

18. (3')(50')(5 1/2') = 825 cu.ft. ≈ 30 cu.yds., since 1 cu.yd. = 27 cu.ft.

19. 7'3 1/2" + 4'2 3/16" + 5'7 5/16" + 8'5 7/8" = 24'17 30/16" = 25'6 7/8"

20. Total expansion = (150)(.0000095)(145)

21. Number of pounds needed = (5) (4)(6-5 1/2)(62) = 620

22. Net annual pay = ($83,125)(.83) ≈ $69000. Then, the net weekly pay = $69000 ÷ 52 ≈ $1325 (actually about $1327)

23. 390 lbs. ÷ 18 = 21.6 lbs. per linear foot

24. (3)(11) = 33 man-days. Then, 33 ÷ 5 = 6.6 ≈ 6 1/2 days

25. Area = (8')(2 1/2') = 20 sq.ft.

READING COMPREHENSION
UNDERSTANDING AND INTERPRETING WRITTEN MATERIAL
EXAMINATION SECTION
TEST 1

DIRECTIONS: Each question or incomplete statement is followed by several suggested answers or completions. Select the one that BEST answers the question or completes the statement. *PRINT THE LETTER OF THE CORRECT ANSWER IN THE SPACE AT THE RIGHT.*

Questions 1-8.

DIRECTIONS: Questions 1 through 8, inclusive, are to be answered in accordance with the following information.

In his 2017 annual report to the Mayor, the Public Works Commissioner stated that the city's basic water pollution control program begun in 1981 and costing $425 million so far would be completed in five or six years at a cost of $275 million more. However, he said, the city must spend an additional $175 million more on its marginal pollution control program to protect present and proposed beaches. Under the basic program, the city will have eliminated the last major discharges of raw sewage into the harbor. Over 800 million gallons, two-thirds of the city's spent water each day, is now treated at 12 plants, to which six new plants will be added, enabling the city to treat the estimated 1.8 billion gallons that will be discharged daily in 2050. The department had about $200 million worth of municipal construction under way in 2017, and completed $85.5 millions' worth.

1. According to the above, the city will add _____ new plants.   1.____

    A. 18   B. 12   C. 6   D. 4

2. The amount of municipal construction under way in 2017 was _____ million.   2.____

    A. $85.5   B. $175   C. $200   D. $425

3. It is estimated that in 2050 the city will treat daily _____ gallons.   3.____

    A. 700 million   B. 800 million   C. 900 million   D. 1.8 billion

4. According to the above article, the total cost of the water pollution program begun in 1981 will be _____ million.   4.____

    A. $275   B. $425   C. $700   D. $815

5. According to the above article, to protect present and proposed beaches, the city must spend an additional _____ million.   5.____

    A. $175   B. $275   C. $425   D. $450

6. The above article concerns the statements of the Commissioner of Public Works in his _____ annual report to the Mayor.   6.____

    A. 1981   B. 2050   C. 2017   D. 2018

7. The word *discharged* as used in the above article means MOST NEARLY   7.____

    A. emitted   B. erased   C. refuted   D. repelled

8. The word *pollution* as used in the above article means MOST NEARLY   8.____

    A. condensation   B. purification
    C. contamination   D. distillation

Questions 9-15.

DIRECTIONS: Questions 9 through 15, inclusive, are to be answered in accordance with the
following information.

At sea level the atmosphere can exert a pressure of 14.7 pounds per square inch. This
pressure is capable of sustaining a column of water having a height equal to 14.7 pounds
multiplied by 2.304 (the height of water in feet which will exert one pound per square inch
pressure). No pump built can produce a perfect vacuum. The atmospheric pressure exerting
its force on the surface of the water from which suction is being taken forces the water up
through the suction to the pump. From this, it is evident that the maximum height which a
water pump of this type can lift water is determined ultimately by the atmospheric pressure.
The tightness of the pump and its ability to create a vacuum also have a bearing.

9. The meaning of the word *vacuum* as used in the above article is a   9.____

    A. space entirely devoid of matter
    B. sealed tube filled with gas
    C. bottle-shaped vessel with a double wall
    D. cleaning device

10. With reference to the above article, if a pump could produce a perfect vacuum, the MAX-   10.____
IMUM height, in feet, that it could lift water at sea level is MOST NEARLY

    A. 33.9   B. 29.4   C. 23.3   D. 14.7

11. With reference to the above article, a column of water having a height of 4.6 feet at sea   11.____
level will exert a pressure of MOST NEARLY _____ pounds per square inch.

    A. 3   B. 2   C. 1   D. $\frac{1}{2}$

12. The word *atmosphere* as used in the above article means   12.____

    A. the pull of gravity
    B. perfect vacuum
    C. the whole mass of air surrounding the earth
    D. the weight of water at sea level

13. The word *bearing* as used in the above article means MOST NEARLY   13.____

    A. direction   B. connection
    C. divergence   D. convergence

14. The word *evident* as used in the above article means MOST NEARLY   14.____

    A. disconcerting   B. obscure
    C. equivocal   D. manifest

15. The word *maximum* as used in the above article means MOST NEARLY   15.____

    A. best   B. median   C. adjacent   D. greatest

Questions 16-19.

DIRECTIONS: Questions 16 through 19, inclusive, are to be answered in accordance with the
               following paragraph.

One of the categories of nuisance is a chemical one and relates to the dissolved oxygen
of the watercourse. The presence in sewage and industrial wastes of materials capable of
undergoing biochemical oxidation and resulting in reduction of oxygen in the watercourse
leads to a partial or complete depletion of this oxygen. This, in turn, leads to the subsequent
production of malodorous products of decomposition, to the destruction of aquatic plant life
and major fish life, and to conditions offensive to sight and smell.

16. The word *malodorous* as used in the above paragraph means MOST NEARLY   16.____

    A. fragrant   B. fetid   C. wholesome   D. redolent

17. From the above paragraph, because of pollution the amount of dissolved oxygen in the   17.____
    waterways is

    A. released   B. multiplied
    C. lessened   D. saturated

18. The word *categories* as used in the above paragraph means MOST NEARLY   18.____

    A. divisions   B. clubs   C. symbols   D. products

19. The word *offensive* as used in the above paragraph means MOST NEARLY   19.____

    A. pliable   B. complaint
    C. deferential   D. disagreeable

Questions 20-22.

DIRECTIONS: Questions 20 through 22, inclusive, are to be answered in accordance with the
               following paragraph.

Thermostats should be tested in hot water for proper opening. A bucket should be filled
with sufficient water to cover the thermostat and fitted with a thermometer suspended in the
water so that the sensitive bulb portion does not rest directly on the bucket. The water is then
heated on a stove. As the temperature of the water passes the 160-165° range, the thermostat should start to open and should be completely opened when the temperature has risen
to 185-190°. Lifting the thermostat into the air should cause a pronounced closing action, and
the unit should be closed entirely within a short time.

20. The thermostat described above is a device which opens and closes with changes in the   20.____

    A. position   B. pressure
    C. temperature   D. surroundings

21. According to the above paragraph, the closing action of the thermostat should be tested   21.____
    by

    A. working the thermostat back and forth
    B. permitting the water to cool gradually
    C. adding cold water to the bucket
    D. removing the thermostat from the bucket

22. The bulb of the thermometer should NOT rest directly on the bucket because   22.____

    A. the bucket gets hotter than the water
    B. the thermometer might be damaged in that position
    C. it is difficult to read the thermometer in that position
    D. the thermometer might interfere with operation of the thermostat

Questions 23-25.

DIRECTIONS: Questions 23 through 25, inclusive, are to be answered in accordance with
              information given in the paragraph below.

All idle pumps should be turned daily by hand and should be run under power at least
once a week. Whenever repairs are made on a pump, a record should be kept so that it will
be possible to judge the success with which the pump is performing its functions. If a pump
fails to deliver liquid, there may be an obstruction in the suction line, the pump's parts may be
badly worn, or the packing defective.

23. According to the above paragraph, pumps   23.____

    A. in use should be turned by hand every day
    B. which are not in use should be run under power every day
    C. which are in daily use should be run under power several times a week
    D. which are not in use should be turned by hand every day

24. According to the above paragraph, the reason for keeping records of repairs made on   24.____
    pumps is to

    A. make certain that proper maintenance is being performed
    B. discover who is responsible for improper repairs
    C. rate the performance of the pumps
    D. know when to replace worn parts

25. The one of the following causes of pump failure which is NOT mentioned in the above   25.____
    paragraph is

    A. excessive suction lift   B. clogged lines
    C. bad packing   D. worn parts

KEY (CORRECT ANSWERS)

1.	C	11.	B
2.	C	12.	C
3.	D	13.	B
4.	C	14.	D
5.	A	15.	D
6.	C	16.	B
7.	A	17.	C
8.	C	18.	A
9.	A	19.	D
10.	A	20.	C

21.	D
22.	A
23.	D
24.	C
25.	A

TEST 2

DIRECTIONS: Each question or incomplete statement is followed by several suggested answers or completions. Select the one that BEST answers the question or completes the statement. *PRINT THE LETTER OF THE CORRECT ANSWER IN THE SPACE AT THE RIGHT.*

Questions 1-2.

DIRECTIONS: Questions 1 and 2 are to be answered in accordance with the information given in the following paragraph.

A sludge lagoon is an excavated area in which digested sludge is desired. Lagoon depths vary from six to eight feet. There are no established criteria for the required capacity of a lagoon. The sludge moisture content is reduced by evaporation and drainage. Volume reduction is slow, especially in cold and rainy weather. Weather and soil conditions affect concentration. The drying period ranges from a period of several months to several years. After the sludge drying period has ended, a bulldozer or tractor can be used to remove the sludge. The dried sludge can be used for fill of low ground. A filled dried lagoon can be developed into a lawn. Lagoons can be used for emergency storage when the sludge beds are full. Lagoons are popular because they are inexpensive to build and operate. They have a disadvantage of being unsightly. A hazard to lagoon operation is the possibility of draining partly digested sludge to the lagoon that creates a fly and odor nuisance.

1. In accordance with the given paragraph, sludge lagoons have the disadvantage of being   1.____

    A. unsightly   B. too deep
    C. concentrated   D. wet

2. In accordance with the given paragraph, moisture content is reduced by   2.____

    A. digestion   B. evaporation
    C. oxidation   D. removal

Questions 3-5.

DIRECTIONS: Questions 3 through 5, inclusive, should be answered in accordance with the following paragraph.

Sharpening a twist drill by hand is a skill that is mastered only after much practice and careful attention to the details. Therefore, whenever possible, use a tool grinder in which the drills can be properly positioned, clamped in place, and set with precision for the various angles. This machine grinding will enable you to sharpen the drills accurately. As a result, they will last longer and will produce more accurate holes.

3. According to the above paragraph, one reason for sharpening drills accurately is that the   3.____
    drills

    A. can then be used in a hand drill as well as a drill press
    B. will last longer
    C. can then be used by unskilled persons
    D. cost less

4. According to the above paragraph,   4.____

    A. it is easier to sharpen a drill by machine than by hand
    B. drills cannot be sharpened by hand
    C. only a skilled mechanic can learn to sharpen a drill by hand
    D. a good mechanic will learn to sharpen drills by hand

5. As used in the above paragraph, the word *precision* means MOST NEARLY   5.____

    A. accuracy   B. ease   C. rigidity   D. speed

Questions 6-9.

DIRECTIONS: Questions 6 through 9, inclusive, should be answered in accordance with the following paragraph.

Centrifugal pumps have relatively fewer moving parts than reciprocating pumps, and no valves. While reciprocating pumps when new are usually more efficient than centrifugal pumps, the latter retain their efficiency longer. Most rotary pumps are also without valves, but they have closely meshing parts between which high pressures may be set up after they begin to wear. In general, centrifugal pumps can be made much smaller than reciprocating pumps giving the same result. There is an exception in that positive displacement pumps delivering small volumes at high heads are smaller than equivalent centrifugal pumps. Centrifugal pumps cost less when first purchased than other comparable pumps. The original outlay may be as little as one-third or one-half that of a reciprocating pump suitable for the same purpose.

6. The type of pump NOT mentioned in the above paragraph is the _____ type.   6.____

    A. rotary   B. propeller
    C. reciprocating   D. centrifugal

7. According to the above paragraph, the type of pump that sometimes has valves and sometimes does NOT is the   7.____

    A. rotary   B. propeller
    C. reciprocating   D. centrifugal

8. According to the above paragraph, centrifugal pumps are   8.____

    A. *always* smaller than reciprocating pumps
    B. *smaller* than reciprocating pumps only when designed to deliver small quantities at low pressures
    C. *larger* than reciprocating pumps only when designed to deliver small quantities at high pressures
    D. *larger* than reciprocating pumps only when designed to deliver large quantities at low pressures

9. The advantage of centrifugal pumps that is NOT mentioned in the above paragraph is that   9.____

    A. the centrifugal pump retains its efficiency longer
    B. it is impossible to create an excessive pressure when using a centrifugal pump

C. there are fewer parts to wear out in a centrifugal pump
D. the centrifugal pump is cheaper

Questions 10-12.

DIRECTIONS: Questions 10 through 12, inclusive, should be answered in accordance with the following paragraph.

Gaskets made of relatively soft materials are placed between the meeting surfaces of hydraulic fittings in order to increase the tightness of the seal. They should be composed of materials that will not be affected by the liquid to be enclosed, nor by the conditions under which the system operates, including maximum pressure and temperature. They should be able to maintain the amount of clearance required between meeting surfaces. One of the materials most widely used in making gaskets is neoprene. Since neoprene is flexible, it is often used in sheet form at points where a gasket must expand enough to allow air to accumulate, as with cover plates on supply tanks. Over a period of time, oil tends to deteriorate the material used in making neoprene gaskets. The condition of the gasket must, therefore, be checked whenever the unit is disassembled. Since neoprene gasket material is soft and flexible, it easily becomes misshapen, scratched or torn. Great care is therefore necessary in handling neoprene. Shellac, gasket sealing compounds or *pipe dope* should never be used with sheet neoprene, unless absolutely necessary for satisfactory installation.

10. Of the following, the one that is NOT mentioned in the above paragraph as a requirement for a good gasket material is that the material must be   10.___

A. cheap
B. unaffected by heat developed in a system
C. relatively soft
D. capable of maintaining required clearances

11. According to the above paragraph, neoprene will be affected by   11.___

A. air   B. temperature   C. pressure   D. oil

12. According to the above paragraph, care is necessary in handling neoprene because   12.___

A. its condition must be checked frequently
B. it tears easily
C. pipe dope should not be used
D. it is difficult to use

Questions 13-15.

DIRECTIONS: Questions 13 through 15, inclusive, are to be answered in accordance with the information given in the paragraph below.

Some gases which may be inhaled have an irritant effect on the respiratory tract. Among them are ammonia fumes, hydrogen sulfide, nitrous fumes, and phosgene. Persons who have been exposed to irritant gases must lie down at once and keep absolutely quiet until the dotor arrives. The action of some of these gases may be delayed, and at first the victim may show few or no symptoms.

13. According to the above paragraph, the part of the body that is MOST affected by irritant gases is the

    A. heart   B. lungs   C. skin   D. nerves

13._____

14. According to the above paragraph, a person who has inhaled an irritant gas should be

    A. given artificial respiration
    B. made to rest
    C. wrapped in blankets
    D. made to breathe smelling salts

14._____

15. A person is believed to have come in contact with an irritant gas but he does not become sick immediately.
According to the above paragraph, we may conclude that the person

    A. did not really come in contact with the gas
    B. will become sick later
    C. came in contact with a small amount of gas
    D. may possibly become sick later

15._____

Questions 16-22.

DIRECTIONS: Questions 16 through 22, inclusive, are to be answered in accordance with the following paragraph.

At 2:30 P.M. on Monday, October 25, Mr. Paul Jones, a newly appointed sewage treatment worker, started on a routine inspectional tour of the settling tanks and other sewage treatment works installations of the plant to which he was assigned. At 2:33 P.M., Mr. Jones discovered a co-worker, Mr. James P. Brown, lying unconscious on the ground. Mr. Jones quickly reported the facts to his immediate superior, Mr. Jack Rota, who immediately tele-phoned for an ambulance. Mr. Rota then rushed to the site and placed a heavy woolen blan-ket over the victim. Mr. Brown was taken to the Ave. H hospital by an ambulance driven by Mr. Dave Smith, which arrived at the sewage disposal plant at 3:02 P.M. Patrolman Robert Daly, badge number 12520, had arrived before the ambulance and recorded all the details of the incident, including the statements of Mr. Jones, Mr. Rota, and Mr. Nick Nespola, a Stationary Engineer (Electric), who stated that he saw the victim when he fell to the ground.

16. The time which elapsed between the start of the sewage treatment worker's routine inspection and the arrival of the ambulance was MOST NEARLY _____ minutes.

    A. 3   B. 28   C. 29   D. 32

16._____

17. The name of the sewage treatment worker's immediate superior was

    A. James P. Brown   B. Jack Rota
    C. Paul Jones   D. Robert Daly

17._____

18. The name of the patrolman was

    A. James P. Brown   B. Jack Rota
    C. Paul Jones   D. Robert Daly

18._____

19. Referring to the above, the incident occurred on   19.____

      A. Monday, Oct. 25   B. Monday, Oct. 26
      C. Tuesday, Oct. 25   D. Tuesday, Oct. 26

20. The victim was found at exactly   20.____

      A. 2:30 A.M.   B. 2:33 P.M.   C. 2:33 A.M.   D. 2:30 P.M.

21. The sewage treatment worker's name was   21.____

      A. James P. Brown   B. Jack Rota
      C. Paul Jones   D. Dave Smith

22. The man named Nick Nespola was the   22.____

      A. Stationary Engineer (Electric)
      B. patrolman
      C. victim
      D. ambulance driver

Questions 23-25.

DIRECTIONS: Questions 23 through 25, inclusive, are to be answered in accordance with the information given in the paragraph below.

The bearings of all electrical equipment should be subjected to careful inspection at scheduled periodic intervals in order to secure maximum life. The newer type of sleeve bearings requires very little attention since the oil does not become contaminated and oil leakage is negligible. Maintenance of the correct oil level is frequently the only upkeep required for years of service with this type of bearing.

23. According to the above paragraph, the MAIN reason for making periodic inspections of   23.____
electrical equipment is to

      A. reduce waste of lubricants
      B. prevent injury to operators
      C. make equipment last longer
      D. keep operators *on their toes*

24. According to the above paragraph, the bearings of electrical equipment should be   24.____
inspected

      A. whenever the equipment isn't working properly
      B. whenever there is time for inspections
      C. at least once a year
      D. at regular times

25. According to the above paragraph, when using newer type of sleeve bearings,   25.____

      A. oil leakage is slight
      B. the oil level should be checked every few years
      C. oil leakage is due to carelessness
      D. oil soon becomes dirty

KEY (CORRECT ANSWERS)

1.	A	11.	D
2.	B	12.	B
3.	B	13.	B
4.	A	14.	B
5.	A	15.	D
6.	B	16.	D
7.	A	17.	B
8.	C	18.	D
9.	B	19.	A
10.	A	20.	B

21.	C
22.	A
23.	C
24.	D
25.	A

TEST 3

DIRECTIONS: Each question or incomplete statement is followed by several suggested answers or completions. Select the one that BEST answers the question or completes the statement. *PRINT THE LETTER OF THE CORRECT ANSWER IN THE SPACE AT THE RIGHT.*

Questions 1-2.

DIRECTIONS: Questions 1 and 2 are to be answered on the basis of the paragraph below.

When summers are hot and dry, much water will be used for watering lawns. Domestic use will be further increased by more bathing, while public use will be affected by much street sprinkling and use in parks and recreation fields for watering grass and for ornamental fountains. Variations in the weather may cause variations in water consumption. A succession of showers in the summer could significantly reduce water consumption. High temperatures may also lead to high water use for air conditioning purposes. On the other hand, in cold weather water may be wasted at the faucets to prevent freezing of pipes, thereby greatly increasing consumption.

1. According to the above passage, water consumption   1.____

    A.   will not be affected by the weather to any appreciable extent
    B.   will always increase in the warm weather and decrease in cold weather
    C.   will increase in cold weather and decrease in warm weather
    D.   may increase because of high or low temperatures

2. The MAIN subject of the above passage is   2.____

    A.   climatic conditions affecting water consumption
    B.   water consumption in arid regions
    C.   conservation of water
    D.   weather variations

Questions 3-4.

DIRECTIONS: Questions 3 and 4 are to be answered on the basis of the paragraph below.

The efficiency of the water works management will affect con-sumption by decreasing loss and waste. Leaks in the water mains and services and unauthorized use of water can be kept to a minimum by surveys. A water supply that is both safe and attractive in quality will be used to a greater extent than one of poor quality. In this connection, it should be recognized that improvement of the quality of water supply will probably be followed by an increase in consumption. Increasing the pressure will have a similar effect. Changing the rates charged for water will also affect consumption. A study found that consumption decreases about five percent for each ten percent increase in water rates. Similarly, water consumption increases when the water rates are decreasing.

3. According to the above passage, an increase in the quality of water would MOST LIKELY   3.___

    A.   cause an increase in water consumption
    B.   decrease water consumption by about 10%

C.   cause a decrease in water consumption
D.   have no effect on water consumption

4.   According to the above passage, a ten percent decrease in water rates would MOST   4.____
     LIKELY result in a _____ in the water consumption.

     A.   five percent decrease   B.   five percent increase
     C.   ten percent decrease   D.   ten percent increase

Questions 5-6.

DIRECTIONS: Questions 5 and 6 are to be answered on the basis of the paragraph below.

While the average domestic use of water may be expected to be about 35 gallons per person daily, wide variations are found. These are largely dependent upon the economic status of the consumers and will differ greatly in various sections of the city. In the high value residential districts of a city or in a suburban community of similar type population, the water consumption per person will be high. In apartment houses, which may be considered as representing the maximum domestic demand to be expected, the average consumption should be about 60 gallons per person. In an area of high value single residences, even higher consumption may be expected since to the ordinary domestic demand there will be added amount for watering lawns. The slum districts of large cities will show a consumption per person of about 20 gallons daily. The lowest figures of all will be found in low value districts where sewerage is not available and where perhaps a single faucet serves one or several households.

5.   According to the above passage, domestic water consump tion per person   5.____

     A.   would probably be lowest for persons in an area of high value single residences
     B.   would probably be lowest for persons in an apartment house
     C.   would probably be lowest for persons in a slum area
     D.   does not depend at all upon area or income

6.   According to the above passage, the water consumption in apartment houses as com-   6.____
     pared to slum houses is about _____ times as much.

     A. $1\frac{1}{2}$ B.   2   C. $2\frac{1}{2}$ D.   3

Questions 7-9.

DIRECTIONS: Questions 7 through 9 are to be answered in accordance with the paragraph below.

A connection for commercial purposes may be made from a metered fire or sprinkler line of 4 inches or larger in diameter, provided a meter is installed on the commercial branch line. Such connection shall be taken from the inlet side of the fire meter control valve, and the method of connection shall be subject to the approval of the department. On a 4-inch fire line, the connection shall not exceed inches in diameter. On a fire line 6 inches or larger in diameter, the size of the connection shall not exceed 2 inches. Fire lines shall not be cross-connected with any system of piping within the building.

7. According to the above paragraph, a connection for commercial purposes may be made to a metered sprinkler line provided that the diameter of the sprinkler line is AT LEAST   7._____

    A. $1\frac{1}{2}$"   B. 2"   C. 4"   D. 6"

8. According to the above paragraph, the connection for commercial purposes is taken from the   8._____

    A. inlet side of the main control valve
    B. outlet side of the wet connection
    C. inlet side of the fire meter control valve
    D. outlet side of the Siamese

9. According to the above paragraph, the MAXIMUM size permitted for the connection for commercial purposes depends on the   9._____

    A. location of the fire meter valve
    B. use to which the commercial line is to be put
    C. method of connection to the sprinkler line
    D. size of the sprinkler line

Questions 10-11.

DIRECTIONS: Questions 10 and 11 are to be answered in accordance with the paragraph below.

Meters shall be set or reset so that they may be easily examined and read. In all premises where the supply of water is to be fully metered, the meter shall be set within three feet of the building or vault wall at. point of entry of service pipe. The service pipe between meter control valve and meter shall be kept exposed. When a building is situated back of the building line or conditions exist in a building that prevent the setting of the meter at a point of entry, meter may be set outside of the building in a proper watertight and frost-proof pit or meter box, or at another location approved by the Deputy Commissioner, Assistant to Commissioner, or the Chief Inspector.

10. According to the above paragraph, a meter should be set   10._____

    A. at a point in the building convenient to the owner
    B. within 3 feet of the building wall
    C. in back of the building
    D. where the district inspector thinks is best

11. According to the above paragraph, one of the conditions imposed when a meter is permitted to be installed outside of a building is that the meter must be installed   11._____

    A. between the service pipe and the meter control valve
    B. within 3 feet of the point of entry of the service pipe
    C. in a watertight enclosure
    D. above ground in a frost-proof box

Questions 12-15.

DIRECTIONS: Questions 12 through 15 are to be answered in accordance with the paragraphs below.

No individual or collective air conditioning system installed on any premises for a single consumer shall be permitted to waste annually more than the equivalent of a continuous flow of five gallons of city water per minute.

All individual or collective air conditioning systems installed on any premises for a single consumer using city water annually in excess of the equivalent of five gallons per minute shall be equipped with a water conserving device such as economizer, evaporative condenser, water cooling tower, or other similar apparatus, which device shall not consume for makeup purposes in excess of 15% of the consumption that would normally be used without such device.

Any individual or collective group of such units installed on any premises for a single consumer with a rated capacity of 25 tons or more, or water consumption of 50 gallons or more per minute, shall be equipped, where required by the department, with a water meter to separately register the consumption of such unit or groups of units.

This rule shall also apply to all air conditioning equipment now in service.

12. The rules described in the above paragraphs apply   12.____

    A. *only* to new installations of air conditioning equipment
    B. *only* to air conditioning systems which waste more than 5 gallons of city water per minute
    C. *only* to new installations of air conditioning equipment which waste more than 5 gallons of city water per minute
    D. to all air conditioning systems, whether existing ones or new installations

13. According to the above paragraphs, one of the acceptable methods of reducing wasting   13.____
of water in an air conditioning system is by means of a

    A. cooling tower   B. water meter
    C. check valve   D. collective system

14. According to the above paragraphs, the department may require that an air conditioning   14.____
system have a separate water meter when the system

    A. wastes more than 5 gallons of city water per minute
    B. uses more than 15% make-up water
    C. is equipped with an economizer
    D. has a rated capacity of 25 tons or more

15. According to the above paragraphs, the MAXIMUM quantity of make-up water permitted   15.____
where an air conditioning system uses 50 gallons of water per minute is _____
gallons/minute.

    A. 7   B. $7\frac{1}{2}$ C. 8   D. $8\frac{1}{2}$

Questions 16-17.

DIRECTIONS: Questions 16 and 17 are to be answered in accordance with the paragraph below.

Where flushometers, suction tanks, other fixtures or piping are equipped with quick closing valves and are supplied by direct street pressure in excess of 70 pounds, an air chamber of an approved type shall be installed within two feet of the house control valve or meter in the service near the point of entry. Where water hammer conditions exist in any installation, regardless of the pressure obtaining, an air chamber of an approved type shall be installed where and as directed by the Chief Inspector or Engineer.

16.   According to the above paragraph, air chambers are required when or wherever   16._____

    A.   there are flushometers
    B.   piping is supplied at a direct street pressure in excess of 70 lbs. per sq. in.
    C.   a quick closing valve is used
    D.   water hammer can occur in any piping

17.   According to the above paragraph, air chambers should be installed   17._____

    A.   within two feet of the house control valve or meter
    B.   in a water system regardless of operating pressure
    C.   on the fixture side of the quick closing valve
    D.   on the suction side of the service meter

Questions 18-23.

DIRECTIONS: Questions 18 through 23 are to be answered in accordance with the paragraph below.

The acceptor's responsibility—The purpose of commercial standards is to establish for specific commodities, nationally *recognized* grades or consumer *criteria* and the benefits therefrom will be measurable in direct proportion to their general recognition and actual use. Instances will occur when it may be necessary to deviate from the standard, and the signing of an acceptance does not *preclude* such departures; however, such signature indicates an *intention* to follow the commercial standard where practicable, in the production, distribution, or consumption of the article in question.

18.   The advantage which may be gained from the establishment of commercial standards is   18._____
dependent upon the

    A.   degree of consumer and manufacturer acceptance
    B.   improvement of product quality
    C.   degree of change required in the manufacturing process
    D.   establishment and use of the highest standards

19.   Nationally respected and adopted commercial standards are   19._____

    A.   *undesirable;* as they are a direct benefit to unscrupulous manufacturers
    B.   *desirable;* as they serve as a yardstick for consumers
    C.   *undesirable;* as they tend to lower quality
    D.   *desirable;* as they tend to reduce manufacturing costs

20. The word *preclude,* as used in this paragraph, means MOST NEARLY   20._____

    A. permit   B. allow   C. include   D. prevent

21. The word *intention,* as used in this paragraph, means MOST NEARLY   21._____

    A. agreement   B. impulse   C. objection   D. obstinance

22. The word *recognized,* as used in this paragraph, means MOST NEARLY   22._____

    A. desirable   B. stable   C. branded   D. accepted

23. The word *criteria,* as used in this paragraph, means MOST NEARLY   23._____

    A. efforts   B. standards   C. usage   D. costs

Questions 24-25.

DIRECTIONS: Questions 24 and 25 are to be answered in accordance with the paragraph below.

Sewage treatment plants are designed so that the sewage flow reaches the plant by gravity. In some instances, a small percentage of the sewerage system may be below the planned level of the plant. Economy in construction and other factors may indicate that the raising of that lower portion of the flow by means of pumps, to the desired plant elevation, is more desirable than lowering the plant structure. Some plants operate with this feature.

24. According to the above paragraph,   24._____

    A. a small percentage of the sewage reaches the plant by means of gravity
    B. all sewage reaches the plant by means of gravity
    C. where sewage cannot reach the plant by gravity, it is pumped
    D. pumping is used so that all sewage can reach the plant

25. According to the above paragraph, the reason that some plants are built above the level of the sewerage system is that   25._____

    A. these plants operate more efficiently this way
    B. gravity will naturally bring the sewage in at a lower level
    C. pumping of the sewage is more expensive
    D. these plants are cheaper to build this way

KEY (CORRECT ANSWERS)

1.	D		11.	C
2.	A		12.	D
3.	A		13.	A
4.	B		14.	D
5.	C		15.	B
6.	D		16.	D
7.	C		17.	A
8.	C		18.	A
9.	D		19.	B
10.	B		20.	D

21.	A
22.	D
23.	B
24.	B
25.	D

———

BASIC PLUMBING

TABLE OF CONTENTS

BASIC PLUMBING

Careful planning and proper installation are essential for a safe and adequate plumbing system in the home or other farmstead buildings.

Installation of plumbing requires special knowledge and tools and should be done by, or under the guidance of, an experienced person. It must be done in accordance with applicable State, county, or local plumbing codes. Code requirements take precedence over recommendations given in this bulletin.

Planning the plumbing system should be done by the family, who know most about their own living habits and needs. A knowledge of the kinds of piping, fixtures, and other equipment required and available will aid in planning. Also, advice should be obtained from qualified persons.

PLANNING

In planning a plumbing system, consider your future needs as well as your present. It costs less to install a few extra tees with plugs for future connections than it does to cut into a plumbing system to make connections later on.

Adding or remodeling plumbing in existing buildings involves the additional expense and labor of opening up walls or floors. It may be more economical to run piping along the exposed face of a wall or floor and then box it in for appearance.

In the home, there are at least three areas where water is needed the kitchen, the bathroom, and the laundry. Around the farmstead, water is needed in the dairy barn and milkhouse. in other buildings where stock are kept or watered, in the shop, and in the yard or family garden. The location of appliances, fixtures, and faucets in each of these areas must be planned in advance.

Planning a plumbing system also includes providing for proper drainage of wastes. Improper handling of wastes can lead to contamination of the water supply and consequent spread of diseases. Poor planning or workmanship can also mean hours of unpleasant work in repairing or clearing clogged drains.

Plumbing costs can often be kept down by good planning in locating fixtures. Fixtures located back to back on opposite sides of a wall, as shown in figure 1 on page 2, save on piping. Locating all bathroom fixtures on one wall, as shown in the illustration, also saves piping. In the arrangement shown in figure 1, one vent stack serves all fixtures.

Figure 2, on page 2, shows a vertical arrangement of fixtures to reduce the amount of piping needed in multi-storied houses. Locating fixtures in a continuous line, as shown in figures 3 and 4, saves piping in single-story houses.

A water heater should be located as close as practical to the fixture where hot water will be used most frequently. Long runs of hot water pipe result in unnecessary use of water and heat.

Precautions

Every precaution must be taken to insure a safe water supply and otherwise protect the health of the family. When installing plumbing, be sure that

- There are no leaks in the drainage system through which sewage or sewer gases can escape.

- There are no cross connections between the water-supply system and any other piping carrying water or other materials.

- All fixtures are designed and installed so that there can be no back siphonage from the fixture into the water-supply system. This precaution also applies to fixtures, such as water bowls, installed in service buildings for use by animals.

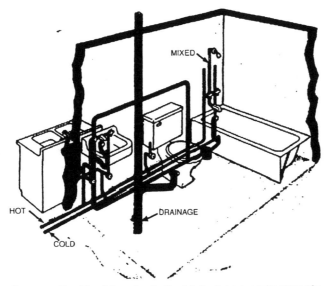

Figure 1 – Plumbing fixtures located back to back on opposite sides of a wall.

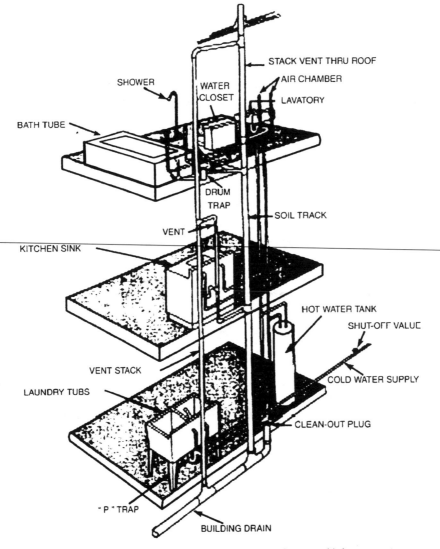

Figure 2 - Plumbing arrangement in a two-story house with basement.

ROUGHING-IN

The term "roughing-in" refers to placing the piping that will be concealed in the walls or under the floors of a building during construction or remodeling. The fixtures are normally connected to this piping after construction work is completed. Future fixtures may also be provided for in this manner.

Building drains may be laid under concrete floors before the superstructure framing is started.

Roughing-in includes installation and testing of the water-supply and drainage piping and the fixture supports. The location and height of sinks, lavatories, and other fixtures must be precisely indicated on the

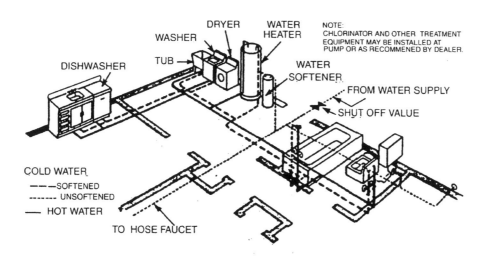

Figure 3 - A fixture and water-supply-piping layout for a one-story house.

building plans to insure correct installation of the piping and supports. For sinks a height of 36 inches and for lavatories a height of 33 to 35 inches, measured from the floor to the top of the rim, should suit most adults. Some families may find it more convenient to have the fixtures slightly higher or lower.

After the roughed-in work is completed, and before it is concealed, the plumbing system should be tested for leaks. Local plumbing codes usually include a standard testing procedure. Where no code is in effect, the drainage and water-supply systems may be tested as follows:

Drainage system–Tightly plug all openings, except the highest one. Fill the system with water, and let the water stand for about 15 minutes. Then check the entire system for leaks.

The system can be checked by sections. If done that way, test each section under a head (depth, measured vertically) of water of at least 10 feet to be sure that each section and joint will withstand at least that much pressure.

Water-supply system–This system can be tested in the same way as the drainage system, but only potable (drinkable) water should be used, and it should be under pressure at least equal to the working pressure of the system, but not less than 60 pounds per square inch. A pump and pressure gage will be needed to make the test.

4

WATER-SUPPLY PIPING

Materials

Galvanized pipe or copper tubing is normally used for water-supply, or distribution piping. However, these two materials should not be joined directly to each other (see p. 12).

Copper tubing may cost a little more than galvanized pipe, but it is easier to install and has a smoother inside surface.

Both hard-drawn (rigid) and soft-drawn (flexible) copper tubing are available. The soft-drawn tubing can be installed with long sweeping bends. Less pressure is lost when water runs through sweeping bends than when it makes abrupt changes in direction.

Characteristics of the water should be considered when selecting piping. Some waters corrode some piping materials. Check with neighbors who use water from the same water-bearing stratum; their experience can guide you in selecting the piping material. Or, have a chemical analysis made of a sample of the water. Your State college or university may be equipped to make an analysis. If not, it can direct you to a private laboratory. Firms in the water treatment equipment business make analyses for prospective customers.

Size

Water-distribution piping should be as short and as straight as possible. The longer the pipe and the smaller its diameter, the greater the loss of pressure. Some pressurew is lost whenever water passes around bends and through elbows and other fittings.

To improve service by providing higher residual pressures, quieter operation, and reduced water hammer, the following water-velocity limits or specific pipe sizes are recommended :

Service mains

Buried lines to buildings: 1¼ inch minimum size pipe; 4 feet per second velocity.

Service branches

Lines serving one or more fixture supply lines: 6 feet per second velocity.

Fixture supply lines

Lines serving individual fixtures, as follows:

Automatic washer, hose bibbs, and wall hydrants: ¾-inch minimum pipe size.

Bathtub, dishwasher, kitchen sink, laundry trays, and shower stall: ½-inch minimum pipe size.

Lavatory and water closet: Check local plumbing code for specific requirements.

DRAINAGE PIPING

The building drainage system includes all piping that carries sewage or other liquid waste to the building sewer, which, in turn, carries it to the disposal facility. Since the escape of sewage or sewer gases can be a serious health hazard, this system must be as carefully designed and installed as the water-distribution system.

A house or building drainage system generally includes these basic parts:

Fixture drain–The piping through which a fixture drains. Each fixture must be trapped and vented.

Fixture branch–A pipe connecting several fixture drains.

Soil stack–The vertical soil pipe into which the water closet or other fixture having a similar function drains, with or without the discharge from other fixtures. It connects to the building drain and is vented up through the roof to the outside air. The vent portion is called the stack vent.

Building drain–The main horizontal drain that receives the discharge from soil, waste, or other drainage pipes inside the building and carries it outside the building to the building sewer, which carries it to the disposal facility.

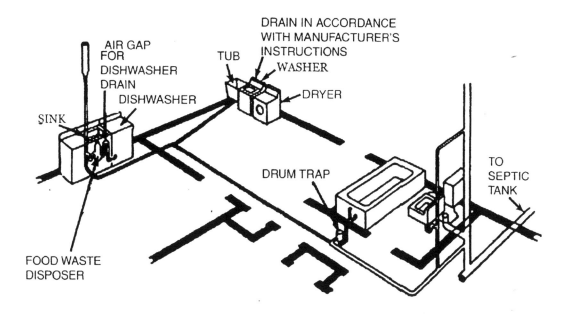

Figure 4 - Drainage system layout for the arrangement in figure 3.

Plastic Piping

Carefully selected and properly installed plastic pipe offers several advantages over conventional piping materials such as galvanized steel and copper pipe or tube. There are no perfect plumbing materials and all must be installed with knowledge of their physical properties and limitations.

Today's plastic pipe and fittings are often the most economical and are nearly immune to the attack of aggressive waters. At this time PE (polyethylene) pipe is used most commonly for underground service. Since it is furnished in long coils, it requires a minimum of fittings for long piping runs. For short runs, the friction loss in the insert fittings is a disadvantage. PVC (polyvinyl-chloride) pipe is available in nearly twice the pressure rating for the same cost as PE. PVC pipe is most often assembled with solvent-welded fittings. Heavy-wall PVC Schedule 80 pipe may be threaded. CPVC (chlorinated-polyvinyl-chloride) pipe is available for hot water service.

ABS (acrilonitrile-butadienestyrene) pipe was once primarily used in potable water distribution in a size known as SWP (solvent-welded pipe). Today ABS is used in DWV (drainage-waste-vent) systems. PVC is also used in DWV systems.

To be sure of getting quality plastic pipe and fittings, make sure that the material is marked with the manufacturer's name or trademark, pipe size, the plastic material type or class code, pressure rating, standard to which the pipe is manufactured (usually an ASTM standard), and the seal of approval of an accredited testing laboratory (usually N.S.F. the National Sanitation Foundation).

Materials

Drainage piping may be made of cast iron, galvanized wrought iron or steel, copper, brass, or plastic. Cast iron is commonly used for building drains that are buried under concrete floors or underground. Steel pipe should not be laid under-ground or under concrete.

Size and Slope

Wastes normally flow through the drainage system by gravity. (Sometimes wastes flow by gravity to a sump, then are lifted by a pump.) The drainage piping must be of the proper size and slope to insure good flow.

Local plumbing codes should be checked for the sizes of drain pipe required. Minimum sizes recommended are:

	Minimum size in inches
Piping for-	
Fixture drains:	
Bathtub, dishwasher, kitchen sink, and laundry trays - - - - -	1½
Lavatory - - - - - - - - - - - - - - - -	1¼
Floor drain and shower stall	2
Water closet - - - - - - - - - - - - -	3
Fixture branch - - - - - - - - - - - - -	1½
Soil stack - - - - - - - - - - - - - - - -	3
Building drain:	
Beyond soil stack connection - -	3
Above soil stack connection - - -	(¹)

¹ Not less than connecting branch.

Horizontal drainpipes—pipes that slope less than 45° from the horizontal—3 inches or less in diameter should slope at least one-fourth of an inch per foot. Larger pipes should slope not less than one-eighth of an men per foot.

Traps and Venting

Gases develop in sewers and septic tanks and flow back through the drainage piping system. To prevent these gases from backing up through open fixture drains or over-flows and escaping into the house, a trap is required at each fixture (figs. 5 and 6). The trap should be the same size as the drainpipe and as close as possible to the fixture outlet. The water seal in the trap should be at least 2 inches, but not more than 4 inches. Water closets usually have built-in traps and no additional one is required. Never double-trap a fixture.

Grease Traps

A grease trap is different from a fixture trap and serves an entirely different purpose. It is designed to prevent greases and fats from entering a sewerage system. It should be used only where large amounts of grease may be discharged into the waste disposal system for example, in a restaurant or boarding house. It is not needed in the average dwelling.

If used, a grease trap should not receive the discharge from a food waste disposer. Grease accumulations must be removed from the trap at frequent intervals.

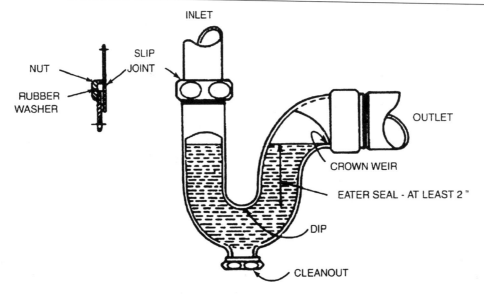

Figure 5 - P trap assembly.

7

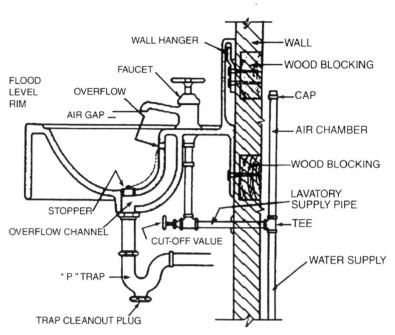

Figure 6 - Lavatory, showing water-supply and drainage piping. Note air gap at faucet and air chamber. An air chamber prevents water hammer.

Drum traps (see fig. 7) are commonly used in bathtub drain lines. A trap should be 3 or 4 inches in diameter, and the bottom or top should be removable to permit cleaning of the trap and drainpipe.

Sewer gases that are confined can develop pressure and bubble through the water seal in fixture traps. Therefore, at least one vent must be provided through which these gases can escape to the outside air and thus prevent any build up of pressure or vacuum on the trap seal.

The soil stack should always be vented to the outside, above the roof and undiminished in size. Additional vents directly to the outside may be needed or required for individual fixtures. Plumbing codes specify the venting required. Where there is no code, the recommendations given herein may be followed.

A vent pipe (or stack, as the vertical portion is called) should extend far enough above the roof to prevent it from being blocked by snow, but at least 6 inches. The opening in the roof through which the pipe passes must be flashed (tightly sealed) to make it watertight (fig. 8).

In very cold climates, the part of a vent above the roof should be at least 3 inches in diameter to prevent frost closure in cold weather. Where individual vents are used for fixtures, 1½-inch pipe is recommended. Vent increasers (see fig. 8) may be used to increase the diameter of the vent stacks above the roof.

Each fixture drain must be vented to prevent the siphoning of the water from the fixture trap. Figures 1, 2, 4, and 7 show the methods of venting fixture drains. Vent piping for each fixture should be installed between the trap and the sewerline, and should be the same size as the drain piping. If connected to the soil stack, the vent piping should be connected above the highest fixture drain. Otherwise, it should extend separately to above the roof. The distance from the fixture trap to the vent is governed by the size of the fixture drain. Maximum distances recommended are:

73

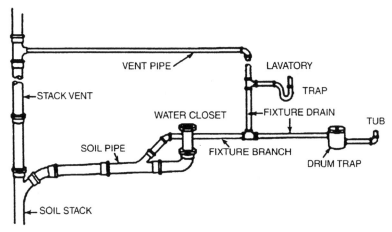

Figure 7 - Method of venting a group of bathroom fixtures.

Size of fixture drain (inches)	Maximum distance from trap to vent (feet)
1¼	2½
1½	3½
2	5
3	6
4	10

It is a good idea to plan the locations of fixtures so that most, if not all, can be vented through one stack. For example, figure 1 shows that by locating the bathroom next to the kitchen, it is practical to vent all fixtures in both rooms through the one stack. This consideration should not necessarily dictate overall room arrangement.

Floor Drains

Floor drains are required in shower stalls, milkrooms, and milking parlors. They are often installed in laundry rooms, basements, and utility rooms.

Floor drains should be trapped. If the building drain is laid under the floor, it must be at a sufficient depth to permit installation of the trap. Floor drains are usually set close enough to the building drain to make separate venting unnecessary.

A floor drain should be flush with the floor, and the floor should slope toward the drain from all directions. The grating of the drain should be removable so the drain can be cleaned.

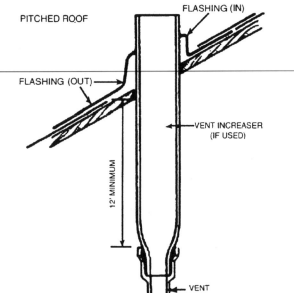

Figure 8 - Installation of roof flashing arround vent stacks.

PIPE FITTINGS AND CLEANOUTS

Fittings

If copper tubing is joined directly to galvanized-iron or steel piping, electrolysis will take place under certain conditions and the joint will eventually corrode. Special non-electrical-conducting fittings are available for joining copper tubing to iron or steel piping.

Pipe fittings, such as elbows, tees, nipples, reducers, and couplings, when used with iron or steel pipes, are usually made of the same material as the pipe. Brass fittings are used with brass pipes and copper tubing.

Valves and faucets are usually made of brass or wrought copper. Brass valves made for use with wrought iron, steel, and rigid copper tubing are threaded; those for use with flexible copper tubing are designed for soldering.

Sections of copper tubing and their fittings are joined by soldering. The soldering should be done as follows:

1. Clean the tube end and the cup (inside) of the fitting with steel wool or emery cloth. Remove all loose particles after cleaning. Clean surfaces are essential for good solder connections.

2. Apply a thin coat of flux to the cleaned surfaces of both the tube and the fitting.

3. Assemble the tube and fitting.

4. Apply heat and solder. Heat by directing the flame onto the fitting toward the tube until the solder melts. The solder will flow and fill the joint.

5. Remove excess flux and solder with a small brush or soft cloth while the metal is still hot.

6. Allow the joint to cool, with-out moving it.

Cast-iron drainage pipe sections and fittings are usually of the hub-and-spigot type and are joined by packing with hemp tow or oakum and sealing with lead (fig. 9). The joint must be fitted and packed so that the sections are concentric, leaving no obstructions to the flow of liquid or projections against which solids can lodge. The direction of waste flow must always be as shown in figure 9.

A recently developed system for joining cast-iron drainage, waste, and vent piping requires only a wrench to assemble. The pipe sections are manufactured without the usual hub and spigot ends and are joined by a neoprene sleeve gasket held in place oy a wrap-around stainless steel shield fastened by stainless steel bands with worm-drive clamps (fig. 10). The absence of hubs enables 2- and 3-inch piping to be installed inside standard 2 x 4's. This method of connection may be used both above and below grade.

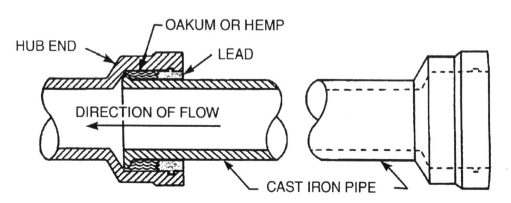

Figure 9 - Bell-and-spigot joint in cast-iron pipe.

Branch drainpipes should be connected to larger drainpipes so that the direction of flow in the system is maintained (see fig. 7).

Where a change in the direction of drainage piping is necessary, sweep bends (fig. 11) should be used whenever possible, because angled turns tend to reduce the rate of flow.

Cleanouts

Wastes that will cling to the inside of pipe walls are sometimes discharged into drainage sytems.

Also, when cool, greases congeal and may stick to pipe walls. To permit cleaning of pipes, cleanouts should be provided through which such matter can be removed or dislodged. Cleanouts usually consist of 45-degree Y-fittings with removable plugs (figs. 11 and 12). They should be the same size as the pipe in which they are installed.

Cleanouts should be installed where they are readily accessible and where cleanout tools can be easily inserted into the drainpipe. Place one cleanout at or near the foot of the soil stack (fig. 13). Install others at intervals of not more than 50 feet along horizontal drainage lines that are 4 inches or less in diameter.

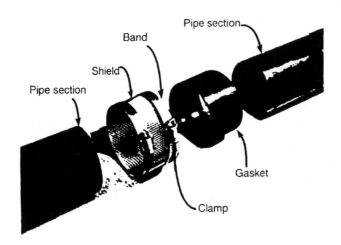

Figure 10 - The newest method of joining pipe is with neoprene gasket shield,and clamps.

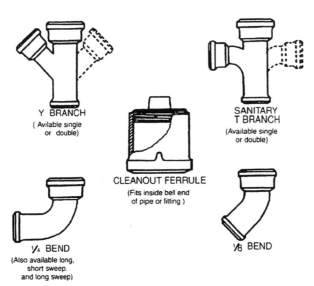

Figure 11 - Common cast-iron soil-pipe fittings.

FIXTURES

Many styles of each type of plumbing fixture are available. Selection is mostly a matter of personal preference. The style and size of a fixture should harmonize with the room in which it is installed.

When designing a new house or building, allow enough space for the desired fixtures. When selecting new fixtures for existing buildings, be sure they will fit into the space available. Draw to scale floor plans of the rooms in which fixtures will be installed (for example, 1/4 or 1/2 inch can equal 1 foot). Arrange cardboard cutouts of the fixtures, drawn to the same scale, on the floor plans.

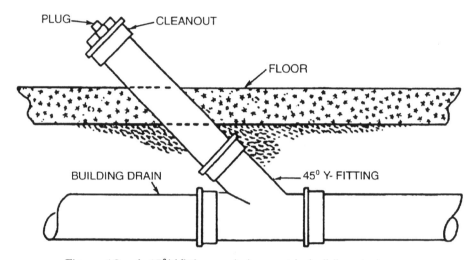

Figure 12 - A 45° Y-fitting and cleanout in building drain.

Manufacturers of plumbing fixtures sometimes have cutouts of their equipment available for planning purposes.

Some plumbing fixtures are supported on the floor alone, some on the wall alone, and some partly on each. Support must be substantial; otherwise a fixture may pull away from the wall and leave a crack. Appropriate carriers or brackets are available for supporting wall-hung fixtures. Guidance on necessary support framing and attachment may be had from fixture manufacturers or dealers.

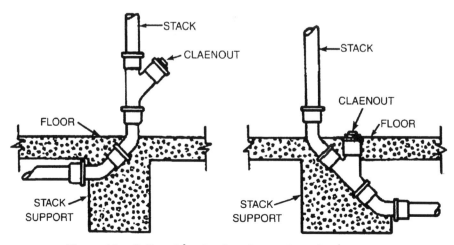

Figure 13 - Soil and waste pipe cleanouts and supports.

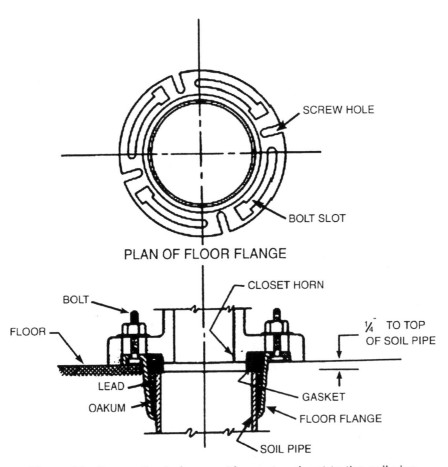

PLAN OF FLOOR FLANGE

Figure 14 - One method of connecting water closet to the soil pipe.

Water closets are available for either floor or wall mounting. The floor-mounted type bolts to a floor flange, which in turn attaches to the floor (fig. 14) or to the closet bend below. The wall-mounted type is supported by carriers attached to the wall studding or to both the wall and the floor (chair carriers). Six-inch wall studding is recommended if wall-type carriers are used. Tubs are available either for floor support alone or for floor and wall support combined, and may require additional framing in the wall or floor, or in both.

Faucet spouts must be high enough above a lavatory or sink rim to prevent water in the fixture from being drawn back into the faucet if a vacuum should be created in the plumbing system. The height, which is known as "air gap," should be at least twice the diameter of the faucet open-

ing (see fig. 6). Normally it should not be less than 1 inch for lavatories; 1 1/2 inches for sinks, laundry trays, and 3/4-inch bath faucets; and 2 inches for 1-inch bath faucets.

Water Treatment

Water for domestic use may require treatment to make it suitable. An analysis will determine the treatment required. Dealers can advise on the selection and use of water-treatment equipment.

Plumbing Check for House Buyers

If you are considering buying a previously occupied house, you should examine and evaluate the condition of the plumbing. The following questions will suggest features that should not be overlooked:

Are there water stains in the building, indicating leaks in the water-supply or drainage piping? If so, have the leaks been corrected satisfactorily?

Is the flow of water from the faucets good and strong, indicating absence of corrosion or scaling in the supply piping? If not, can the deficiency be corrected economically?

Do the fixtures drain quickly and quietly and maintain the water seals in the traps, indicating an adequate vented drainage system? If not, can the deficiency be corrected economically?

Are all fixtures and piping firmly anchored or supported!

Does the water closet flush completely and shut off completely? Does the tank refill quietly? If not, can the deficiency be corrected economically?

Do faucets and valves operate freely and close completely? If not, can the deficiency be corrected economically?

Are the fixtures chipped and stained? Do they need to be replaced?

Do the stoppers hold? If not, can they be readily and cheaply replaced or repaired?

WATER HEATERS

A house plumbing system usually includes a water heater or a hot-water storage tank if the water is heated in the central heating plant. (Water heaters are also required in milkhouses, see p. 16.)

Electric, gas, and oil-fueled water heaters are available. Each type comes in a wide variety of sizes. Instructions for connecting water heaters to plumbing systems come with the units. The tanks have the necessary internal piping already installed and the only connections required are the hot- and cold-water and fuel lines. Gas- or oil-fired water heaters require flues to vent the products of combustion.

Pressure and temperature relief valves are essential and should be on all water heaters and hot-water storage tanks. Their purpose is to relieve pressure in the tank and pipes if other control equipment fails and the water temperature goes high enough to generate dangerous pressure. As water heats it expands, and the expansion may be enough to rupture the tank or pipes if the water cannot be forced back into the cold-water line or discharged through a relief outlet.

The size of hot-water storage tank needed in the house depends upon the number of persons in the family, the volume of hot water that may be required during peak use periods (for example, during bathing or laundering periods), and the "recovery rate" of the heating unit. Household water heaters are generally available with tanks in a range of sizes from about 30 to 80 gallons.

The "recovery rate" of water heaters varies with the type and capacity of the heating element. In standard conventional models, oil and gas heaters usually have higher recovery rates than electric heaters of similar size. However, a relatively new "quick recovery" type of electric water heater is available. Its two high-wattage heating elements provide hot water at a rapid rate.

For a family of 4 or 5 persons, tank sizes should be about 30 to 40 gallons for oil or gas heaters, 40 gallons for quick-recovery electric heaters, and 40 to 52 gallons for standard electric heaters. For larger families, or where unusually heavy use will be made of hot water, correspondingly larger capacity heaters should be installed. Advice on the size needed may be obtained from Extension home demonstration agents, equipment dealers, and power company representatives. Power suppliers may offer special reduced rates for electric water heating. If "off peak" electric heating will be used, be sure that the tank will hold enough hot water to last from one heating period to the next.

PROTECTING WATER PIPES FROM FREEZING

If water freezes in a pipe, the pipe may be ruptured or otherwise damaged.

Freezing will not occur if a pipe is well insulated (fig. 15) and the water is allowed to flow continuously. However, insulation does not stop the loss of heat it merely reduces the rate of loss and the water may freeze if it stands in a pipe, even a well-insulated one, for some time in cold weather.

Pipes laid in the ground are usually difficult to insulate effectively because of moisture; insulation must stay dry to be effective. But a pipe laid below the frostline is not likely to freeze even if not insulated.

In areas subject to freezing temperatures, it is advisable not to install water pipes in outside walls of buildings. Should it be necessary to do so, they should be protected from freezing.

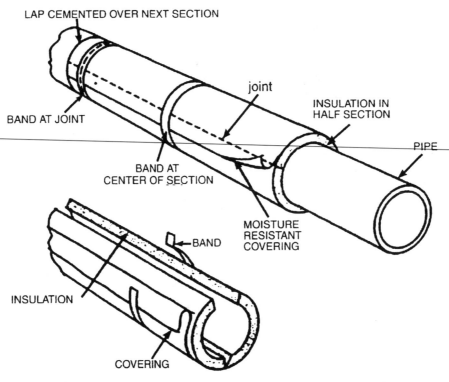

Figure 15 - One method of applying insulation to pipe

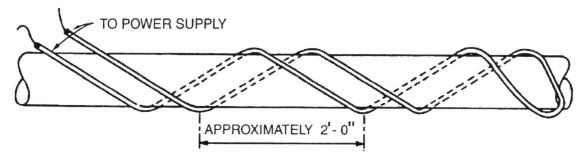

Figure 16 - Application of heating cable to pipe to prevent freezing

Electric heating cable can be used to prevent pipes from freezing. Each unit of cable should be folded at the midpoint and wrapped around the pipe as shown in figure 16. Electric heating cable may also be used to thaw frozen pipe.

CONDENSATION

In areas where the air gets hot and humid, condensation (sweating) is very likely to occur on pipes carrying cold water. This can be prevented by insulating the pipes. The insulation will also help to keep the water cool. To prevent condensation from collecting in the insulation, it should be covered with a good vapor barrier. Vapor barriers are ordinarily available from the same sources as the insulation.

Condensation may also occur on a water-closet tank in hot, humid weather. This may be prevented by insulating the tank. Insulating jackets, or liners, that fit inside water-closet tanks are available. When installed, they prevent the water from cooling the outer surface of the tank.

SERVICE-BUILDING PLUMBING

Water-Supply Piping

Water is needed in all buildings and yards where livestock are kept.

In stall-type dairy barns, water is usually provided by means of water bowls. The bowls must be designed to prevent back siphoning of water into the water-supply piping. This may be done by using valves with outlets above the overflow rim of the bowl (fig. 17).

The supply piping for water bowls is often mounted on the stall frame where it may be subject to freezing. Freezing can be prevented by wrapping heating cable around the pipe, and covering the cable and pipe with insulation (figs. 15 and 16). If the pipe is laid underground, the riser to the bowl must be protected against freezing.

Precautions against back siphoning of water into the supply piping and against freezing must also be taken with troughs and other types of stock waterers. Heating devices are available to prevent freezing.

Where there is danger of the pipes freezing in service buildings, a stop-and-waste valve should be installed between the building service pipe and the distribution piping. The valve, which may be buried in the ground where the service pipe enters the building, will permit draining the piping in the building during cold weather. When the valve handle, which extends above the ground, is closed, the water in the service pipe drains through an opening in the valve

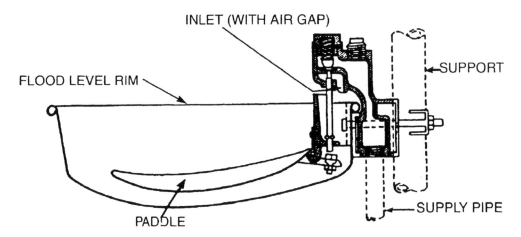

INLET (WITH AIR GAP)

FLOOD LEVEL RIM

SUPPORT

SUPPLY PIPE

PADDLE

Figure 17 - Livestock watering bowl.

into the ground. If the ground around the valve is not sufficiently porous to absorb the drainage, it should be made so by packing with gravel or broken stone.

In cold climates, outdoor faucets should be the frostproof type. Frostproof hydrants are designed to drain the water left in them when they are turned off. This prevents freezing.

Water is needed for washing down stall barns and milking parlors. Both hot and cold water should be provided in the operator area of milking parlors for washing udders, rinsing pails, and other cleaning.

Hot and cold water are required in the milkhouse or milk room.

Note: Consult your dairy inspector regarding regulations before installing milkhouse plumbing. A water heater should be included in the milkhouse plumbing system. Water heaters for the dairy are usually larger than those used for household water heating and may operate at a higher temperature. On large dairy farms where a considerable amount of equipment must be washed and sterilized, a steam boiler may be advisable.

Hose connections or other outlets should be provided for flushing paved livestock feeding and resting areas.

Drainage Piping

Proper handling and disposal of dairy building wastes—especially from the gutters in stall barns, in milking parlors, and in milk rooms-is essential to prevent contamination of dairy products. Local health authorities should be consulted when planning a dairy waste-disposal system. All requirements in the milk code must be followed.

Milkhouse drainage systems must be adequate to carry away the waste water from washing utensils, the milk-cooling equipment, and the milkhouse. In small milkhouses, one 4-inch drain may be adequate; in larger ones, two drains may be needed-one under the washing vat and one in the center of the floor. The milkhouse wastes should not drain into the household sewage-disposal system, but into a separate system. Milkhouse drains should be trapped and vented; the method is the same as for house drains.

Your milk code may require a washroom with a lavatory and water closet for use by the dairy help. Wastes from this washroom are sewage and should not drain into the milkhouse or barn waste-disposal systems. Either provide a separate disposal system or, if practical, use the household sewage-disposal system.

SIMPLE PLUMBING REPAIRS

TABLE OF CONTENTS

SIMPLE PLUMBING REPAIRS

• Repairing water faucets and valves.

• Repairing leaks in pipes and tanks.

• Thawing frozen pipes.

• Repairing water closets.

• Cleaning clogged drains.

Extensive plumbing repairs or alterations in the plumbing system usually require authorization from local authorities and possibly inspection of the completed work. Therefore such work should be done by a qualified or licensed plumber.

REPAIRING WATER FAUCETS AND VALVES

Faucets and globe valves, the type of shutoff valves commonly used in home water systems, are very similar in construction (fig. 1) and repair instructions given below apply to both. Your faucets or valves may differ somewhat in general design from the one shown in figure 1, because both faucets and valves come in a wide variety of styles.

Mixing faucets, which are found on sinks, laundry trays, and bathtubs, are actually two separate units with a common spout. Each unit is independently repaired.

If a faucet drips when closed or vibrates ("sings" or "flutters") when opened, the trouble is usually the washer at the lower end of the spindle. If it leaks around the spindle when opened, new packing is needed. To replace the washer

• Shut off the water at the shutoff valve nearest the particular faucet.

• Disassemble the faucet the handle, packing nut, packing, and spindle, in that order. You may have to set the handle back on the spindle and use it to unscrew and remove the spindle.

• Remove the screw and worn washer from the spindle. Scrape all the worn washer parts from the cup and install a new washer of the proper size.

• Examine the seat on the faucet body. If it is nicked or rough, reface it. Hardware or plumbing-supply stores carry the necessary seat-dressing tool. *Hold the tool vertically when refacing the seat.*

• Reassemble the faucet. Handles of mixing faucets should be in matched positions.

To replace the packing, simply remove the handle, packing nut, and old packing, and install a new packing washer. If a packing washer is not available, you can wrap stranded graphite-asbestos wicking around the spindle. Turn the packing nut down tight against the wicking.

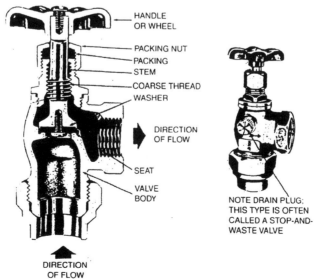

Figure 1 – **Globe-type angle valve. Faucets are similar in construction.**

Other faucet parts may be replaced as necessary.

Complete faucet, inserts in which the washer does not turn on the seat are available. This feature prolongs washer life indefinitely.

Several new faucet designs aimed at easier operation, eliminating drip, and promoting long service life, are on the market. Instructions for repair may be obtained from dealers.

If a shower head drips, the supply valve has not been fully closed, or the valve needs repair.

After extended use and several repairs, some valves will no longer give tight shutoff and must be replaced. When this becomes necessary, it may be advisable to upgrade the quality with equipment having better flow characteristics and longer-life design and materials. In some cases, ball valves will deliver more water than globe valves. Some globe valves deliver more flow than others for identical pipe sizes. Y-pattern globe valves, in straight runs of pipe, have better flow characteristics than straight stop valves. Figure 2 shows the features of different types of valves.

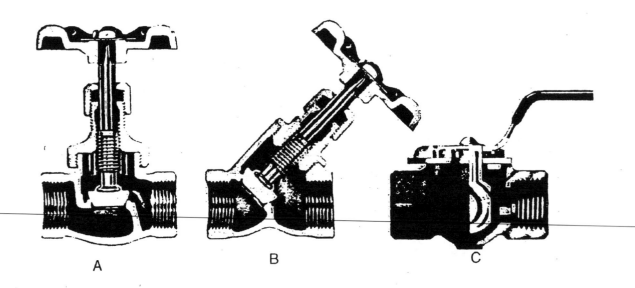

A   B   C

Figure 2.-Different types of valves: *A,* Straight-thru globe valve; note large passages for water. *B,* Y-pattern globe valve; the flow is almost straight. *C,* Ball valve; some makes are available with the port in the ball the same diameter as the pipe.

PRECAUTIONS

Polluted water or sewage may carry such diseases as typhoid fever and amoebic dysentery. If you do your own plumbing work, be sure that

• There are no leaks in drainpipes through which sewage or sewage gases can escape.

• There are no cross connections between piping carrying water from different sources unless there can be reasonable certainty that all sources are safe and will remain safe.

• There can be no back siphonage of water from plumbing fixtures or other containers into the water-supply system.

Once a pipe has become polluted, it may be difficult to f reo it of the pollution. For this reason, building codes do not permit the use of second-hand pipe. All initial piping and parts and subsequent replacements should be new.

Since a plumbing system will require service from time to time, shutoff valves should be installed at strategic locations so that an affected portion can be isolated (water flow to it cut off) with minimum disturbance to service in the rest of the system. Shutoff valves are usually provided on the water closet supply line, on the hot- and cold-water supply line to each sink, tub, and lavatory, and on the water heater supply line. Drain valves are usually installed for water-supply piping systems and for hot-water storage tanks.

A pressure-relief valve should be installed for the water heater storage tank to relieve pressure buildup in case of overheating.

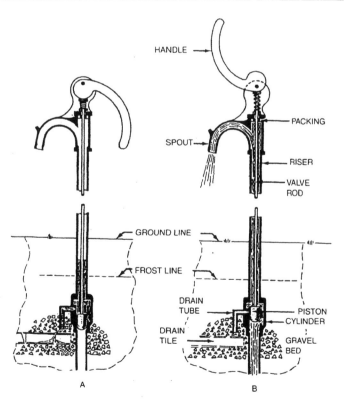

Figure 3.-Frostproof hydrant; A, Closed; B, opened. As soon as the hydrant is closed, water left in the riser drains out the drain tube as shown in A. This prevents water from freezing in the hydrant in cold weather.

FROSTPROOF HYDRANTS

Frostproof hydrants are basically faucets, although they may differ somewhat in design from ordinary faucets.

Two important features of a frostproof hydrant are: (1) The valve is installed under ground-below the frostline-to prevent freezing, and (2) the valve is designed to drain the water from the hydrant when the valve is closed.

Figure 3 shows one type of frostproof hydrant. It works as follows: When the handle is raised, the piston rises, opening the valve. Water flows from the supply pipe into the cylinder, up through the riser, and out the spout. When the handle is pushed down, the piston goes down, closing the valve and stopping the flow of water. Water left in the hydrant flows out the drain tube into a small gravel-filled dry well or drain pit.

As with ordinary faucets, leakage will probably be the most common trouble encountered with frostproof hydrants. Worn packing, gaskets, and washers can cause leakage. Disassemble the hydrant as necessary to replace or repair these and other parts.

Frostproof yard hydrants having buried drains can be health hazards. The vacuum created by water flowing from the hydrant may draw in contaminated water standing above the hydrant drain level. Such hydrants should be used only where positive drainage can be provided.

Frostproof wall hydrants (fig. 4) are the preferred type. For servicing sprayers using hazardous chemicals, hydrants having backflow protection should be used (fig. 5).

① 1/2" OR 3/4"GATE VALVE
② 1/2" OR 3/4" SCH. 40.GALV.
③ 1/2" OR 3/4" VACUUM BREAKER
④ 1/2" OR 3/4" ELL.M.I.GALV.
⑤ EXTERIOR BUILDING WALL
⑥ 1" SLEEVE, SCH.40
⑦ HANDWHEEL
⑧ IPS HOSE ADAPTER
⑨ COUPLING M.I. GALV.
⑩ 1/2" OR 3/4" NIPPLE GALV.

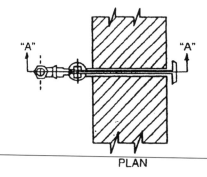

PLAN

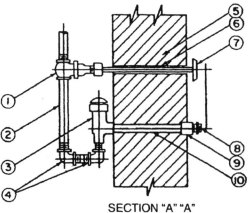

SECTION "A" "A"

Figure 4 – **Vacuum breaker arrangement for outside hose hydrant.**

REPAIRING LEAKS IN PIPES AND TANKS

PIPES

Leaks in pipes usually result from corrosion or from damage to the pipe. Pipes may be damaged by freezing, by vibration caused by machinery operating nearby, by water hammer, or by animals bumping into the pipe. (Water hammer is discussed on P. 8)

Corrosion

Occasionally waters are encountered that corrode metal pipe and tubing. (Some acid soils also corrode metal pipe and tubing.)

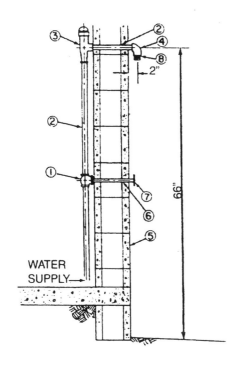

WATER SUPPLY→

① 3/4" BALL OR GATE VALVE
② 3/4" PIPE, GALV
③ 3/4" VACUUM BREAKER
④ 3/4" ELL. M.L. GALV.
⑤ EXTERIOR BUILDING WALL
⑥ 1" SLEEVE
⑦ VALVE HANDLE
⑧ HOSE ADAPTER

***Figure 5* – Protected wall hydrant suitable for filling agricultural sprayers.**

The corrosion usually occurs, in varying degrees, along the entire length of pipe rather than at some particular point. An exception would be where dissimilar metals, such as copper and steel, are joined.

Treatment of the water may solve the problem of corrosion. Otherwise, you may have to replace the piping with a type made of material that will be less subject to the corrosive action of the water.

It is good practice to get a chemical analysis of the water before selecting materials for a plumbing system. Your State college or university may be equipped to make an analysis; if not, you can have it done by a private laboratory.

Repairing Leaks

Pipes that are split by hard freezing must be replaced.

A leak at a threaded connection can often be stopped by unscrewing the fitting and applying a pipe joint compound that will seal the joint when the fit-ing is screwed back together.

Small leaks in a pipe can often be repaired with a rubber patch and metal clamp or sleeve. This must be considered as an emergency repair job and should be followed by permanent repair as soon as practicable.

Large leaks in a pipe may require cutting out the damaged section and installing a new piece of pipe. At least one union will be required unless the leak is near the end of the pipe. You can make a temporary repair with plastic or rubber tubing. The tubing must be strong enough to withstand the normal water pressure in the pipe. It should be slipped over the open ends of the piping and fastened with pipe clamps or several turns of wire.

Vibration sometimes breaks solder joints in copper tubing, causing leaks. If the joint is accessible, clean and resolder it. The tubing must be dry before it can be heated to soldering temperature. Leaks in places not readily accessible usually require the services of a plumber and sometimes of both a plumber and a carpenter.

Tanks

Leaks in tanks are usually caused by corrosion. Sometimes, a safety valve may fail to open and the pressure developed will spring a leak.

While a leak may occur at only one place in the tank wall, the wall may also be corroded thin in other places. Therefore, any repair should be considered as temporary, and the tank should be replaced as soon as possible.

A leak can be temporarily repaired with a toggle bolt, rubber gasket, and brass washer, as shown in figure 6. You may have to drill or ream the hole larger to insert the toggle bolt. Draw the bolt up tight to compress the rubber gasket against the tank wall.

WATER HAMMER

Water hammer sometimes occurs when a faucet is suddenly closed. When the flow of water is suddenly stopped, its kinetic energy is expended against the walls of the piping. This causes the piping to vibrate, and leaks or other damage may result.

Water hammer may be prevented or its severity reduced by installing an air chamber just ahead of the faucet. The air chamber may be a piece of air-filled pipe or tubing, about 2 feet long, extending vertically from the pipe. It must be airtight. Commercial devices designed to pre-water hammer are also available.

An air chamber requires occasional replenishing of the air to prevent it from becoming water-logged-that is, full of water instead of air.

A properly operating hydro-pneumatic tank, such as the type used in individual water systems, serves as an air chamber, preventing or reducing water hammer.

FROZEN WATER PIPES

In cold weather, water may freeze in underground pipes laid above the frostline or in pipes in unheated buildings, in open crawl spaces under buildings, or in outside walls.

When water freezes it expands. Unless a pipe can also expand, it may rupture when the water freezes. Iron pipe and steel pipe do not expand appreciably. Copper pipe will stretch some, but does not resume its original dimensions when thawed out; repeated freezings will cause it to fail eventually. Flexible plastic tubing can stand repeated freezes, but it is good practice to prevent it from freezing.

Preventing Freezing

Pipes may be insulated to prevent freezing, but this is not a completely dependable method. Insulation does not stop the loss of heat from the pipemerely slows it downand the water may freeze if it stands in the pipe long enough at below-freezing temperature. Also, if the insulation becomes wet, it may lose its effectiveness.

Electric heating cable can be used to prevent pipes from freezing. The cable should be wrapped around the pipe and covered with insulation.

Thawing

Use of electric heating cable is a good method of thawing frozen pipe, because the entire heated length of the pipe is thawed at one time.

Thawing pipe with a blowtorch can be dangerous. The water may get hot enough at the point where the torch is applied to generate sufficient steam under pressure to rupture the pipe. Steam from the break could severely scald you.

Thawing pipe with hot water is safer than thawing with a blowtorch. One method is to cover the pipe with rags and then pour the hot water over the rags.

When thawing pipe with a blowtorch, hot water, or similar methods, open a faucet and start thawing at that point. The open faucet will permit steam to escape, thus reducing the chance of the buildup of dangerous pressure. Do not allow the steam to condense and refreeze before it reaches the faucet.

Underground *metal* pipes can be thawed by passing a low-voltage electric current through them. The current will heat the entire length of pipe through which it passes. Both ends of the pipe must be open to prevent the buildup of steam pressure.

CAUTION: This method of thawing frozen pipe can be dangerous and should be done by an experienced person only. It cannot be used to thaw plastic tubing or other non-electricity-conducting pipe or tubing.

REPAIRING WATER CLOSETS

Water closets (commonly called toilets) vary in general design and in the design of the flushing mechanism. But they are enough alike that general repair instructions can suffice for all designs.

Flushing Mechanism

Figure 7 shows a common type of flushing mechanism. Parts that usually require repair are the flush valve, the intake (float) valve, and the float ball.

In areas of corrosive water, the usual copper flushing mechanism may deteriorate in a comparatively short time. In such cases, it may be advisable to replace the corroded parts with plastic parts. You can even buy plastic float balls.

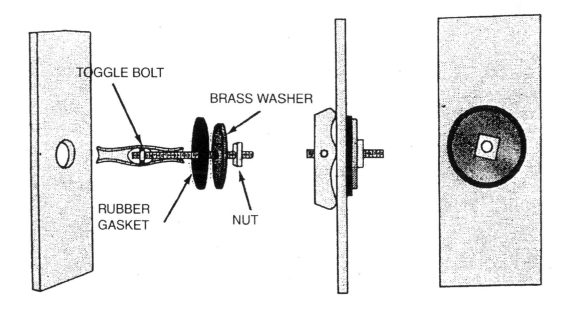

Figure 6.-Closing a hole in a tank: *A,* The link of the toggle bolt is passed through the hole in the tank (hole is enlarged if necessary). *B.* Side view of tank edge (nut is drawn up tightly to compress washer and gasket against tank). *C,* Outside view of completed repair.

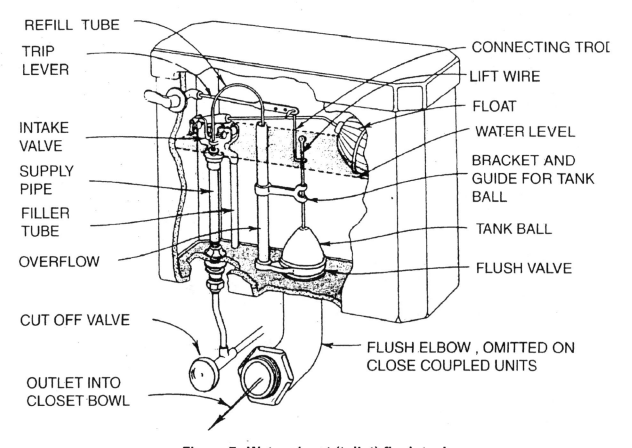

REFILL TUBE

TRIP LEVER

INTAKE VALVE

SUPPLY PIPE

FILLER TUBE

OVERFLOW

CUT OFF VALVE

OUTLET INTO CLOSET BOWL

CONNECTING TROD

LIFT WIRE

FLOAT

WATER LEVEL

BRACKET AND GUIDE FOR TANK BALL

TANK BALL

FLUSH VALVE

FLUSH ELBOW , OMITTED ON CLOSE COUPLED UNITS

Figure 7. **Water closet (toilet) flush tank.**

Flush Valve

The rubber ball of the flush valve may get soft or out of shape and fail to seat properly. This causes the valve to leak. Unscrew the ball from the lift wire and install a new one.

The trip lever or lift wire may corrode and fail to work smoothly, or the lift wire may bind in the guides. Disassemble and clean off corrosion or replace parts as necessary.

Most plumbing codes require a cutoff valve in the supply line to the flush tank, which makes it unnecessary to close down the whole system (fig. 7). If this valve was not installed, you can stop the flow of water by propping up the float with a piece of wood. Be careful not to bend the float rod out of alignment.

Intake (Float) Valve

A worn plunger washer in the supply valve will cause the valve to leak. To replace the washer-
• Shut off the water and drain the tank.
• Unscrew the two thumbscrews that hold the levers and push out the levers.
• Lift out the plunger, unscrew the cup on the bottom, and insert a new washer. The washer is made of material such as rubber or leather.
• Examine the washer seat. If nicked or rough, it may need refacing.

If the float-valve assembly is badly corroded, replace it.

Float Ball

The float ball may develop a leak and fail to rise to the proper position. (Correct water level is about 1 inch below the top of the overflow tube or enough to give a good flush.) If the ball fails to rise, the intake valve will remain open and water will continue to flow.

Brass float balls can sometimes be drained and the leak soldered. Other types must be replaced. When working on the float ball, be careful to keep the rod alined so that the ball will float freely and close the valve properly.

BOWL REMOVAL

An obstruction in the water closet trap or leakage around the bottom of the water-closet bowl may require removal of the bowl. Follow this procedure:

• Shut off the water.

• Empty the tanl- and bowl by siphoning or sponging out the water.

• Disconnect the water pipes to the tank (see fig. 7).

• Disconnect the tank from the bowl if the water closet is a two-piece unit. Set the tank where it cannot be damaged. Handle tank and bowl carefully; they are made of vitreous china or porcelain and are easily chipped or broken.

• Remove the seat and cover from the bowl.

• Carefully pry loose the bolt covers and remove the bolts holding the bowl to the floor flange (fig. 8). Jar the bowl enough to break the seal at the /bottom. Set the bowl upside down on something that will not chip or break it.

• Remove the obstruction from the discharge opening.

• Place a new wax seal around the owl horn and press it into place. A wax seal (or gasket) may be obtained from hardware or plumbing-supply stores.

• Set the bowl in place and press it down firmly. Install the bolts that hold it to the floor flange. Draw the bolts up snugly, but not too tight because the bowl may break. The bowl must be level. Keep a carpenter's level on it while drawing up the bolts. If the house has settled, leaving the floor sloping, it may be necessary to use shims to make the bowl set level. Replace the bolt covers.

• Install the tank and con- nect the water pipes to it. It is advisable to replace all

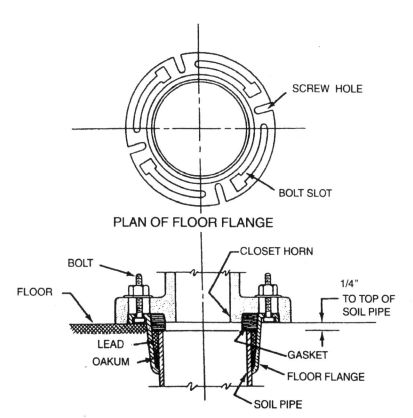

Figure 8 – Connection of water closet to floor and soil pipe.

gaskets, after first cleaning the surfaces thoroughly.

• Test for leaks by flushing a few times.

• Install the seat and cover.

Tank "Sweating"

When cold water enters a water closet tank, it may chill the tank enough to cause "sweating" (condensation of atmospheric moisture on the outer surface of the tank). This can be prevented by insulating the tank to keep the temperature of the outer surface above the dew point temperature of surrounding air. Insulating jackets or liners that fit inside water-closet tanks and serve to keep the outer surface warm are available from plumbing-supply dealers.

CLEARING CLOGGED DRAINS

Drains may become clogged by objects dropped into them or by accumulations of grease, dirt, or other matter.

Fixture and Floor Drains

If the obstruction is in a fixture trap, usually the trap can be removed and cleared. If the obstruction is elsewhere in the pipe other means must be used.

Cleanout augers-long, flexible, steel cables commonly called "snakes"-may be run down drainpipes to break up obstructions or to hook onto and pull out objects. Augers are made in various lengths and diameters and are available at hardware and plumbing-supply stores. (In some cases, you may have to call a plumber, who will probably have a power-driven auger.)

Small obstructions can sometimes he forced down or drawn up by use of an ordinary rubber force cup (plunger or "plumber's friend").

Grease and soap clinging to a pipe can sometimes be removed by flushing with hot water. Lye or lye mixed with a small amount of aluminum shavings may also be used. When water is added to the mixture, the violent gas-forming reaction and production of heat that takes place loosens the grease and soap so that they can be flushed away. *Use cold water only.* Chemical cleaners should not be used in pipes that are completely stopped up, because they must be brought into direct contact with the stoppage to be effective. Handle the material with extreme care and follow directions on the container. If lye spills on the hands or clothing, wash with cold water immediately. If any gets into the eyes, flush with cold water and call a doctor.

Sand, dirt, or clothing lint sometimes clogs floor drains. Remove the strainer and ladle out as much of the sediment as possible. You may have to carefully chip away the concrete around the strainer to free it. Flush the drain with clean water. If pressure is needed, use a garden hose. Wrap cloths around the hose where it enters the drain to prevent backflow of water. You may have to stand on this plug to keep it in place when the water is turned on.

Occasional flushing of floor drains may prevent clogging.

CAUTION: Garden hoses, augurs, rubber force cups, and other tools used in direct contact with sewage are subject to contamination. Do not later use them for work on your potable water supply system unless they have been properly sterilized.

Outside Drains

Roots growing through cracks or defective joints sometimes clog outside drains or sewers. You can clear the stoppage temporarily by using a root-cutting tool. However, to prevent future trouble, you should re-lay the defective portion of the line, using sound pipe and making sure that all joints are watertight.

If possible, sewer lines should be laid out of the reach of roots. But if this is impossible or impracticable, consider using impregnated fiber pipe which tends to repel roots.

TOOLS AND SPARE PARTS

Basic tools that you should have on hand to make simple plumbing repairs include:

Wrenches, including pipe wrenches, in a range of sizes to fit the pipe, fittings, fixtures, equipment, and appliances in the system.

Screwdrivers in a range of sizes to fit the faucets, valves, and other parts of the system.

Ball peen hammer or a 12- or 16-ounce clawhammer.

Rubber force cup (plunger or "plumber's friend").

Cold chisel and center punch.

Cleanout auger ("snake").

Friction tape.

Adjustable pliers.

Additional tools required for more extensive plumbing repairs include:

Pipe vise.

Set of pipe threading dies and stocks.

Hacksaw and blades (blades should have 32 teeth per inch).

Pipe cutter, roller type.

Tapered reamer or half-round file.

Carpenter's brace.

Set of wood bits.

Gasoline blowtorch.

Lead pot and ladle.

Calking tools.

Copper tube cutter with reamer (if you have copper tubing).

Always use the proper size wrench or screwdriver. Do not use pipe wrenches on nuts with flat surfaces; use an adjustable or open-end wrench. Do not use pipe wrenches on polished-surface tubings or fittings, such as found on plumbing fixtures; use a strap wrench. Tight nuts or fittings can sometimes be loosened by tapping lightly with a hammer or mallet.

When cutting pipe with a hacksaw, insert the pipe through a block of hard wood as shown in figure 9. A slot sawed in the block guides the saw during the cutting.

It should not be necessary to stock a large number of spare parts. Past plumbing troubles may give some indication as to the kind of parts most likely to be needed. Spare parts should include:

Faucet washers and packing.

One or two lengths of the most common type and size of piping in the plumbing system.

Several unions and gaskets or unions with ground surfaces.

Several couplings and elbows.

A few feet of pipe strap.

An extra hose connection.

EMERGENCIES

Grouped below are emergencies that may occur and the action to take. The name, address, and phone number of a plumber who offers 24-hour service should be posted in a conspicuous place.

Burst pipe or tank. — Immediately cut off the flow of water by closing the shutoff valve nearest to the break. Then arrange for repair.

Water closet overflow.— Do not use water closet until back in working order. Check for and remove stoppage in closet bowl outlet, drain line from closet to sewer, or sewer or septic tank. If stoppage is due to root entry into pipe, repair of pipe at that point is recommended.

Rumbling noise in hot water tank.— This is likely a sign of overheating which could lead to the development of explosive pressure (Another indication of overheating is hot water backing up in the cold-water supply pipe.) Cut off the burner immediately. Be sure that the pressure-relief valve is operative. Then check (with a thermometer) the temperature of the water at the nearest outlet. If above that for which the gage is set, check the thermostat that con-

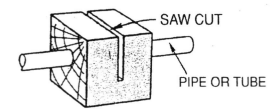

SAW CUT

PIPE OR TUBE

trols burner cutoff. If you cannot correct the trouble, call a plumber.

Cold house. — If the heating system fails (or if you close the house and turn off the heat) when there is a chance of sub-freezing weather, completely drain the plumbing system. A drain valve is usually provided at the low point of the water supply piping for this purpose. A pump, storage tank, hot-water tank, water closet tank, water-treatment apparatus, and other water-system appliances or accessories should also be drained. Put antifreeze in all fixture and drain traps.

Hot-water and steam heating systems should also be drained when the house temperature may drop below freezing.

GLOSSARY OF PLUMBING TERMS

TABLE OF CONTENTS

GLOSSARY OF PLUMBING TERMS

A

ACCEPTED STANDARDS

Accepted standards are the standards cited in the manual, or other standards approved by the authority having jurisdiction over plumbing.

AIR GAP

The air gap in a water-supply system for plumbing fixtures is the vertical distance between the supply-fitting outlet (spout) and the highest possible water level in the receptor when flooded.

If the plane at the end of the spout is at an angle to the surface of the water, the mean gap is the basis for measurement.

APPROVED

Approved means accepted as satisfactory to the authority having jurisdiction over plumbing.

AREA DRAIN

An area drain is a drain installed to collect surface or rain water from an open area.

B

BACKFLOW

Backflow means the flow of water into a water-supply system from any source except its regular one. Back siphonage is one type of backflow.

BACKFLOW CONNECTION

A backflow connection is any arrangement whereby backflow can occur.

BACK VENT

A back vent is a branch vent installed primarily for the purpose of protecting fixture traps from self-siphonage.

BRANCH

A branch is any part of a piping system other than a main. (See Main.)

BRANCH INTERVAL

A branch interval is a length of soil or waste stack corresponding in general to a story height, but in no case less than 8 feet, within which the horizontal branches from one floor or story of the building are connected to the stack.

BRANCH VENT

A branch vent is any vent pipe connecting from a branch of the drainage system to the vent stack.

BUILDING DRAIN

The building (house) drain is that part of the lowest horizontal piping of a building-drainage system which receives the discharge from soil, waste, and other drainage pipes inside the walls of the building and conveys it to the building (house) sewer beginning 5 feet outside the inner face of the building wall.

BUILDING-DRAINAGE SYSTEM
The building-drainage system consists of all piping provided for carrying waste water, sewage, or other drainage from the building to the street sewer or place of disposal.

BUILDING MAIN
The building main is the water-supply pipe including fittings and accessories, from the water (street) main or other source of supply to the first branch of the water-distributing system.

BUILDING SEWER
The building (house) sewer is that part of the horizontal piping of a building-drainage system extending from the building drain 5 feet outside of the inner face of the building wall to the street sewer or other place of disposal (a cesspool, septic tank, or other type of sewage-treatment device or devices) and conveying the drainage of but one building site.

BUILDING SUBDRAIN
A building (house) subdrain is that portion of a drainage system which cannot drain by gravity into the building sewer.

C

CIRCUIT VENT
A circuit vent is a group vent extending from in front of the last fixture connection of a horizontal branch to the vent stack.

COMBINATION FIXTURE
Combination fixture is a trade term designating an integral combination of one sink and one or two laundry trays in one fixture.

CONTINUOUS-WASTE-AND-VENT
A continuous-waste-and-vent is a vent that is a continuation of and in a straight line with the drain to which it connects. A continuous-waste-and-vent is further defined by the angle of the drain and vent at the point of connection make with the horizontal; for example, vertical continuous-waste-and-vent, 45 continuous-waste-and-vent, and flat (small angle) continuous-waste-and-vent.

CONTINUOUS WASTE
A waste from two or more fixtures connected to a single trap.

CROSS-CONNECTION
See: INTERCONNECTION

D

DEVELOPED LENGTH

The developed length of a pipe is its length along the center line of the pipe and fittings.

DIAMETER

Unless specifically stated, the term diameter means the nominal diameter as designated commercially.

DISTANCE

The distance or difference in elevation between two sloping pipes is the distance between the intersection of their center lines with the center line of the pipe to which both are connected.

DOUBLE OFFSET

A double offset is two offsets installed in succession or series in the same line.

DRAIN

A drain or drain pipe is any pipe which carries water or waterborne wastes in a building-drainage system.

DRAINAGE PIPING

Drainage piping is all or any part of the drain pipes of a plumbing system.

DRY VENT

A dry vent is any vent that does not carry water or water-borne wastes.

DUAL VENT

A dual vent (sometimes called a unit vent) is a group vent connecting at the junction of two fixture branches and serving as a back vent for both branches.

E

EFFECTIVE OPENING

The effective opening is the minimum cross-sectional area between the end of the supply-fitting outlet (spout) and the inlet to the controlling valve or faucet. The basis of measurement is the diameter of a circle of equal cross-sectional area.

If two or more lines supply one outlet, the effective opening is the sum of the effective openings of the individual lines or the area of the combined outlet, whichever is the smaller.

F

FIXTURE BRANCH

A fixture branch is the supply pipe between the fixture and the water-distributing pipe.

FIXTURE DRAIN

A fixture drain is the drain from the trap of a fixture to the junction of the drain with any other drain pipe.

FIXTURE UNIT

A fixture unit is a factor so chosen that the load-producing values of the different plumbing fixtures can be expressed approximately as multiples of that factor.

FLOOD LEVEL

Flood level in reference to a plumbing fixture is the level at which water begins to overflow the top or rim of the fixture.

G

GRADE

The grade of a line of pipe is its slope in reference to a horizontal plane. In plumbing it is usually expressed as the fall in inches per foot length of pipe.

GROUP VENT

A group vent is a branch vent that performs its functions for two or more traps.

H

HORIZONTAL BRANCH

A horizontal branch is a branch drain extending laterally from a soil or waste stack or building drain, with or without vertical sections or branches, which receives the discharge from one or more fixture drains and conducts it to the soil or waste stack or the building (house) drain.

I

INDIRECT WASTE PIPE

An indirect waste pipe is a waste pipe which does not connect directly with the building-drainage system, but discharges into it through a properly trapped fixture or receptacle.

INTERCONNECTION

An interconnection, as the term is used is any physical connection or arrangement of pipes between two otherwise separate building water-supply systems whereby water may flow from one system to the other, the direction of flow depending upon the pressure differential between the two systems.

Where such connection occurs between the sources of two such systems and the first branch from either, whether inside or outside the building, the term cross-connection (American Water Works terminology) applies and is generally used.

J

JUMPOVER
See: RETURN OFFSET.

L

LEADER
A leader or downspout is the water conductor from the roof to the storm drain or other means of disposal.

LOOP VENT
A loop vent is the same as a circuit vent except that it loops back and connects with a soil- or waste-stack vent instead of the vent stack.

M

MAIN
The main of any system of continuous piping is the principal artery of the system to which branches may be connected.

MAIN VENT
See: VENT STACK.

N

NONPRESSURE DRAINAGE
Nonpressure drainage refers to a condition in which a static pressure cannot be imposed safely on the building drain. This condition is sometimes referred to as gravity flow and implies that the sloping pipes are not completely filled.

O

OFFSET
An offset in a line of piping is a combination of elbows or bends which brings one section of the pipe out of line with but into a line parallel with another section.

P

PLUMBING
Plumbing is the work or business of installing in buildings the pipes, fixtures, and other apparatus for bringing in the water supply and removing liquid and water-borne wastes. The term is also used to denote the installed fixtures and piping of a building.

PLUMBING FIXTURES
Plumbing fixtures are receptacles which receive and discharge water, liquid, or water-borne wastes into a drainage system with which they are connected.

PLUMBING SYSTEM
The plumbing system of a building includes the water-supply distributing pipes; the fixtures and fixture traps; the soil, waste, and vent pipes; the building (house) drain and building (house) sewer; and the storm-drainage pipes; with their devices, appurtenances, and connections all within or adjacent to the building.

POOL
A pool is a water receptacle used for swimming or as a plunge or other bath, designed to accommodate more than one bather at a time.

PRESSURE DRAINAGE

Pressure drainage, as used in the manual, refers to a condition in which a static pressure may be imposed safely on the entrances of sloping building drains through soil and waste stacks connected thereto.

PRIMARY BRANCH

A primary branch of the building (house) drain is the single sloping drain from the base of a soil or waste stack to its junction with the main building drain or with another branch thereof.

R

RELIEF VENT

A relief vent is a branch from the vent stack, connected to a horizontal branch between the first fixture branch and the soil or waste stack, whose primary function is to provide for circulation of air between the vent stack and the solid or waste stack.

RETURN OFFSET

A return offset or jumpover is a double offset installed so as to return the pipe to its original line.

RISER

A riser is a water-supply pipe which extends vertically one full story or more to convey water to branches or fixtures.

S

SAND INTERCEPTOR (SAND TRAP)

A sand interceptor (sand trap) is a watertight receptacle designed and constructed to intercept and prevent the passage of sand or other solids into the drainage system to which it is directly or indirectly connected.

SANITARY SEWER

A sanitary sewer is a sewer designed or used only for conveying liquid or water-borne waste from plumbing fixtures.

SECONDARY BRANCH

A secondary branch of the building drain is any branch of the building drain other than a primary branch.

SEWAGE-TREATMENT PLANT

A sewage-treatment plant consists of structures and appurtenances which receive the discharge of a sanitary drainage system, designed to bring about a reduction in the organic and bacterial content of the waste so as to render it less offensive or dangerous, including septic tanks and cesspools.

SIDE VENT

A side vent is a vent connecting to the drain pipe through a 45° wye.

SIZE OF PIPE AND TUBING

The size of pipe or tubing, unless otherwise stated, is the nominal size by which the pipe or tubing is commercially designated. Actual dimensions of the different kinds of pipe and tubing are giver in the specifications applying.

SOIL PIPE

A soil pipe is any pipe which conveys the discharge of water closets or fixtures having similar functions, with or without the discharges from other fixtures.

STACK

Stack is a general term for the vertical main of a system of soil, waste, or vent piping.

STACK-VENT

A stack-vent is the extension of a soil or waste stack above the highest horizontal or fixture branch connected to the stack.

STORM DRAIN

A storm drain is a drain used for conveying rain water, subsurface water, condensate, cooling water, or other similar discharges.

STORM SEWER

A storm sewer is a sewer used for conveying rain water, subsurface water, condensate, cooling water, or other similar discharges.

SUBSOIL DRAIN

A subsoil drain is a drain installed for collecting subsurface or seepage water and conveying it to a place of disposal.

T

TRAP

A trap is a fitting or device so designed and constructed as to provide a liquid trap seal which will prevent the passage of air through it.

TRAP SEAL

The trap seal is the vertical distance between the crown weir and the dip of the trap.

V

VENT

A vent is a pipe installed to provide a flow of air to or from a drainage system or to provide a circulation of air within such system to protect trap seals from siphonage and back pressure.

VENT STACK

A vent stack, sometimes called a main vent, is a vertical vent pipe installed primarily for the purpose of providing circulation of air to or from any part of the building-drainage system.

W

WASTE PIPE

A waste pipe is a drain pipe which receives the discharge of any fixture other than water closets or other fixtures receiving human excreta.

WATER MAIN

The water (street) main is a water-supply pipe for public or community use.

WATER-SERVICE PIPE

The water-service pipe is that part of a building main installed by or under the jurisdiction of a water department or company.

WATER-SUPPLY SYSTEM

The water-supply system of a building consists of the water-service pipe, the water-distributing pipes, and the necessary connecting pipes, fittings, and control valves.

WET VENT

A wet vent is a soil or waste pipe that serves also as a vent.

Y

YOKE VENT

A yoke vent is a vertical or 45° relief vent of the continuous-waste-and-vent type formed by the extension of an upright wye-branch or 45° wye-branch inlet of the horizontal branch to the stack. It becomes a dual yoke vent when two horizontal branches are thus vented by the same relief vent.
